Treasured Drawings from Mark Catesby

A Coloring Book for all Ages

By Adalene M. Wood

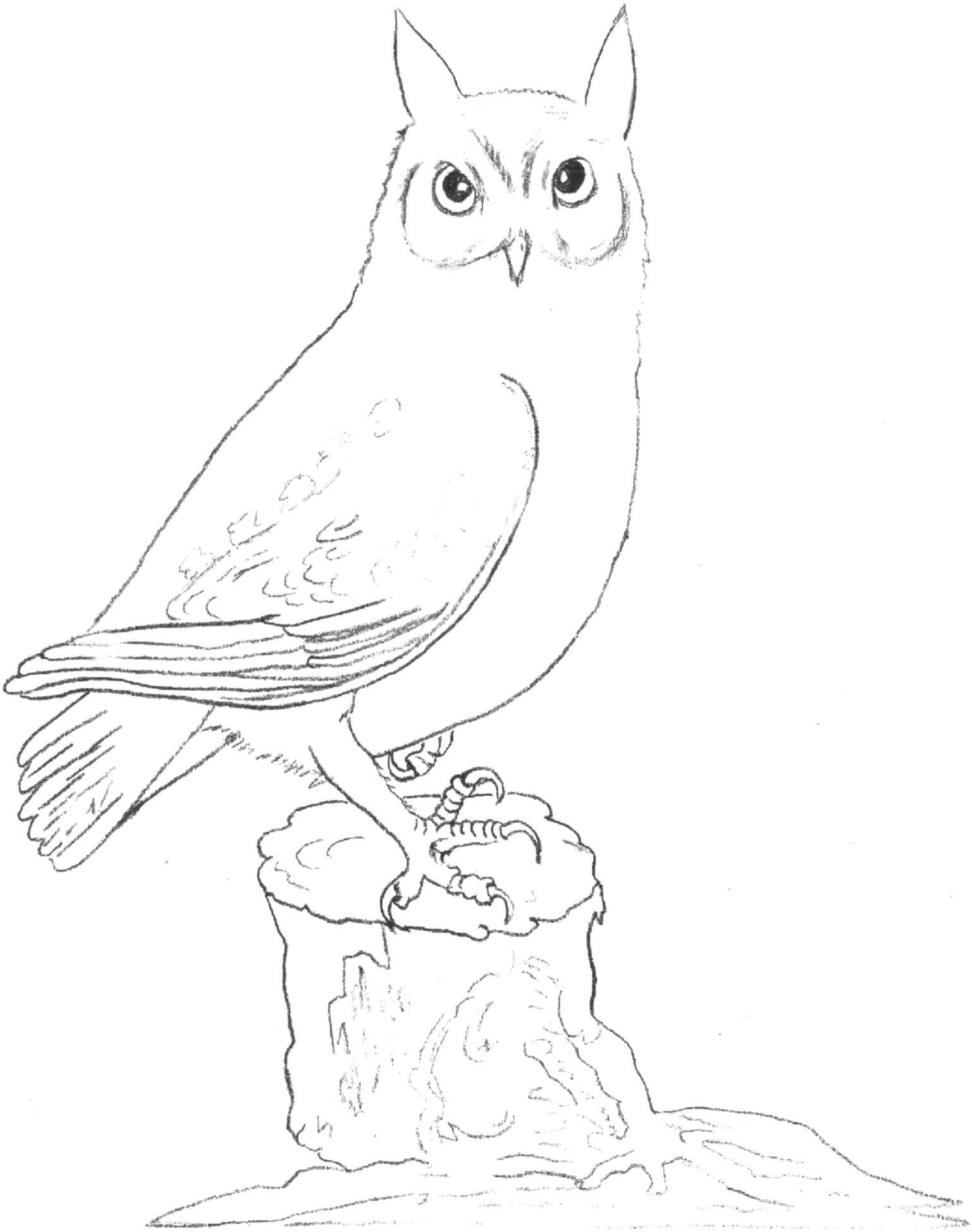

This book was created for the Cocke-Catesby Reunion 2015 which was held in Charleston, SC, October 8-10. We hope that children of all ages will enjoy coloring the beautiful and precise drawings of Mark Catesby.

Foreword about Mark Catesby

On April 22, 1712 Mark Catesby first arrived in Virginia. He made the voyage from England to accompany his sister, Elizabeth Catesby Cocke, who was joining her husband, Dr. William Cocke, at their new home in Williamsburg. Mark stayed as a guest of friends for some years. He became keenly interested in documenting the flora and fauna of the New World. When he returned to England, he sought and received financial support from the Royal Society of London to continue his scientific endeavors. In 1722 Mark sailed to South Carolina and began the arduous task of describing and accurately drawing wildlife he observed in the Carolinas, Florida and the Bahamas. Mark Catesby returned to England in 1726. For three years he worked to compile his drawings and research into a book. It was a high honor when Mark Catesby was presented to the British Royal Court in May 1729. He gave his book, The Natural History of Carolina, Florida and the Bahama Islands, to Queen Caroline. Today his book remains a prized possession of the Royal Collection at Windsor Castle.

To
Isabelle, Charles and James

**Mark Catesby wildlife images are courtesy of Biodiversity Heritage Library. Digitized by Smithsonian Libraries. www.biodiversitylibrary.org

All written text and illustrations rendered in this book were created by Adalene M. Wood, except illustrations on pages 17 and 21. © 2015 by Adalene M. Wood.
ISBN-13: 978-1517048020

Special thanks to Jessica Wood, Andrew Frueh and Claire Blancher for their contributions to this book.

Introduction

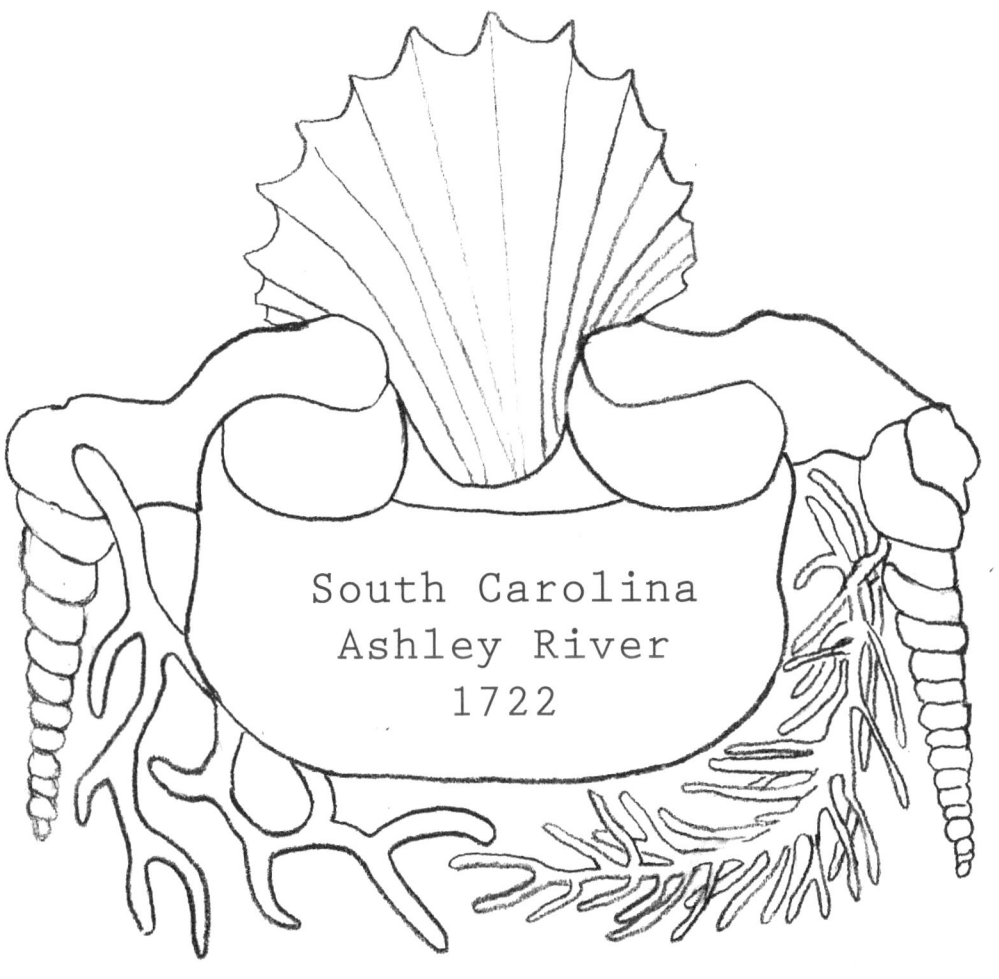

South Carolina
Ashley River
1722

Mark Catesby's plan was to sketch and color
animals and birds that he would discover;
then he would send them to the Queen,
showing her the New World pristine!

Mr. Catesby's Carolina Canoe Trip
A Story told by Mister F. Squirrel

One warm Carolina day in 1722,
I saw Mark in a cypress canoe.
His guide suddenly turned the canoe with his oar.
I watched from my branch as they landed on shore.

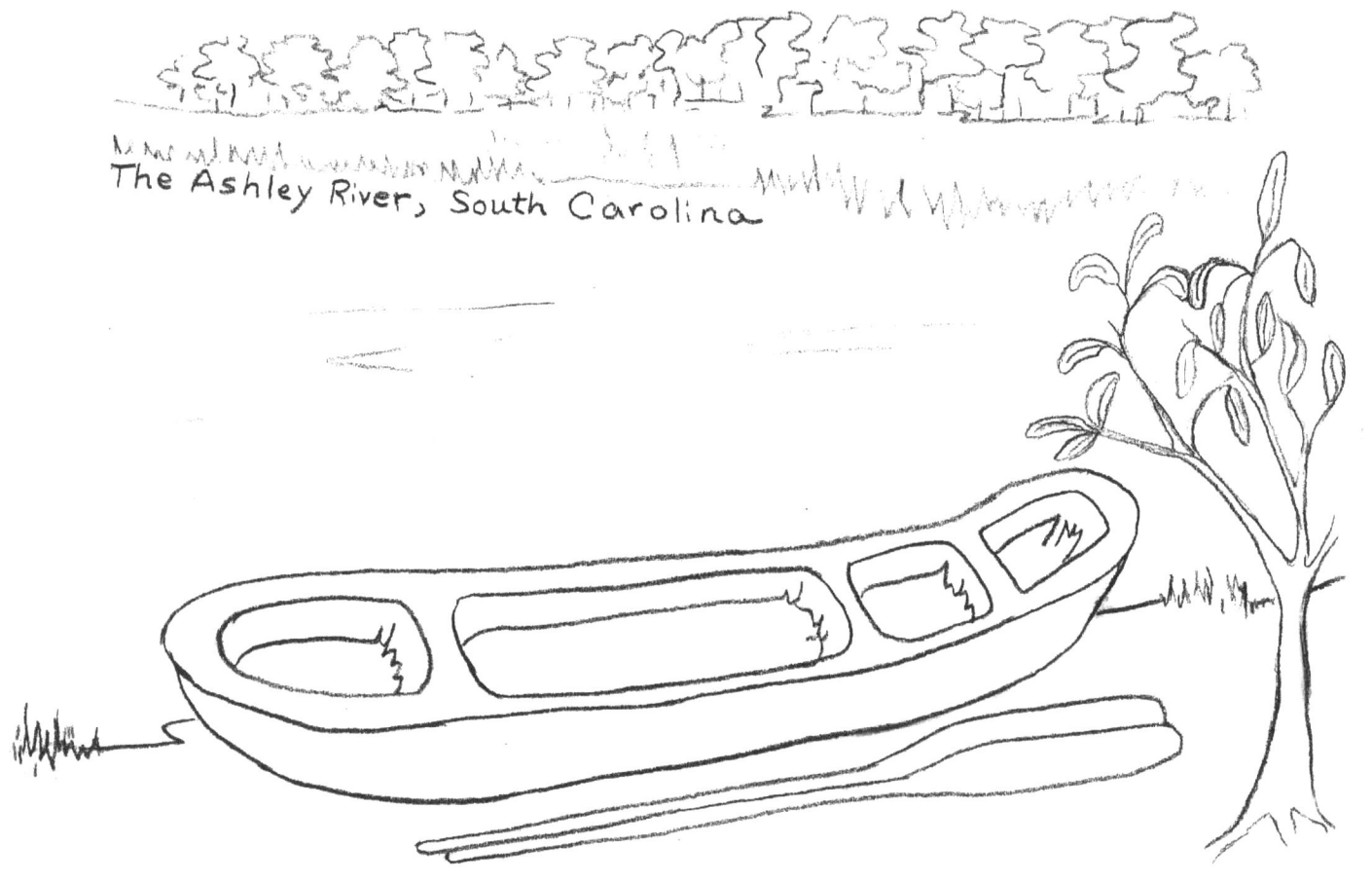

The Ashley River, South Carolina

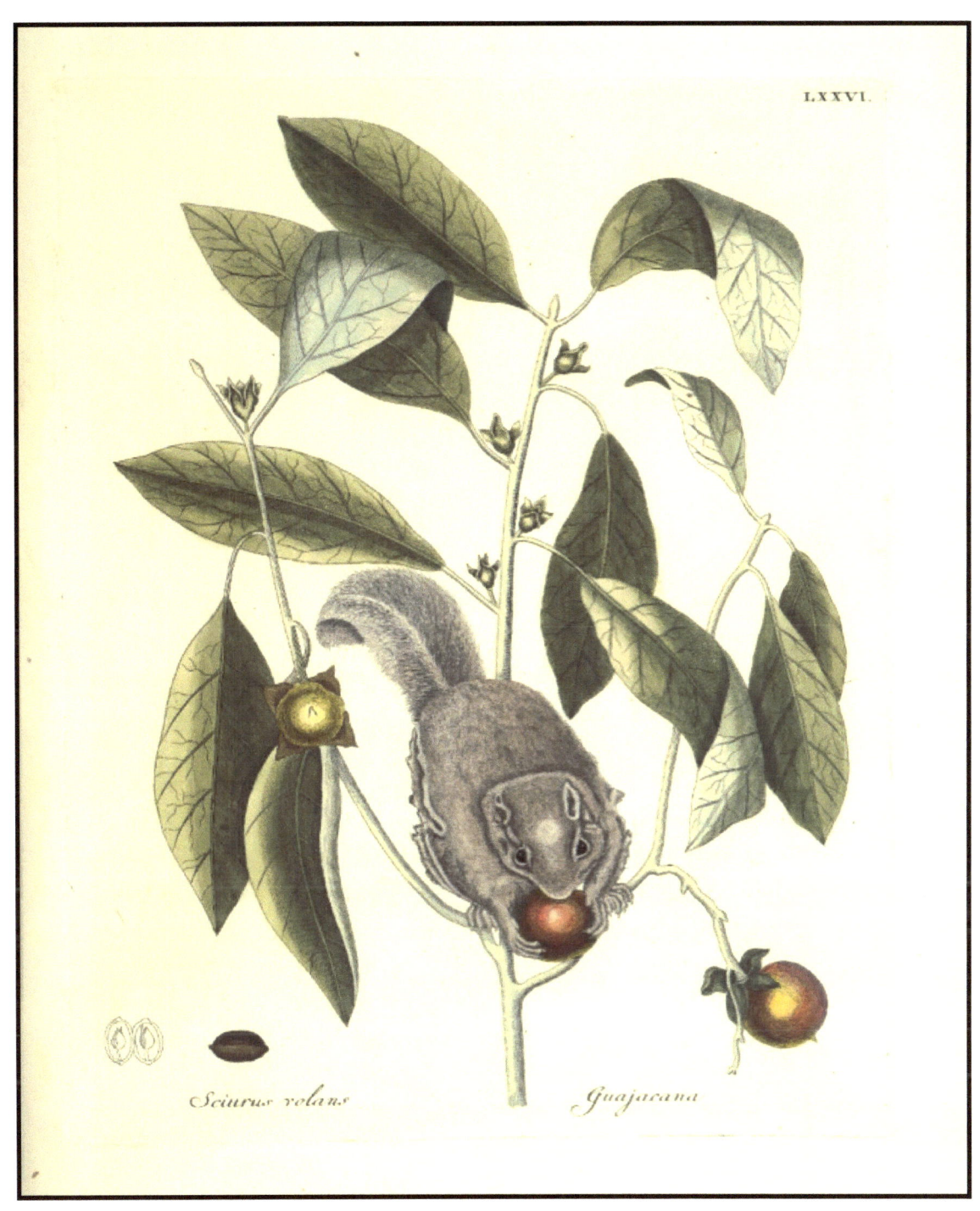

Mark drew my picture when I was about to eat
a delicious persimmon--my favorite treat!
Amazed at my high gliding and flaps that unfurl,
he recorded my achievements and named me
"Flying Squirrel"!

Below are "Flying Squirrel" facts Mark wrote in his book. He described perfectly my handsome look!

I watched as he filled his canoe more and more with treasured drawings no one had seen before.

The Flying Squirrel.

THIS is about the Size of the Ground Squirrel, but has a somewhat shorter Body and Head: The Ears were round, the Eyes black, and large; the Body covered with very fine Hair, as soft, tho' longer than that of a Mole, of a light Mouse Dun Colour: The Tail long, broad, and flat, the Hairs of it exceeding fine and soft.

These Squirrels have not membranous Wings like those of a Bat, whereby they can fly to any great Distance, but have only Membranes, covered with their Furr, which grow along their Sides, and are attached to their Legs, by which they can expand them, and so help themselves in leaping from one Tree to another, as I shall mention in the following Page.

These Species of Squirrels hath been lately discovered in *Poland*, an accurate Description and Print thereof, communicated by the ingenious and curious Mr. *Klein*, Secretary to the City of Dantzick is published in the *Philosophical Transactions*, N° 427. p. 32.

My forest had no hotels, no shelters of any kind,
no telephones or soft beds--just thickets and vines!
Sometimes it rained. Sometimes the wind blew.
Where did Mark sleep? What did he do?

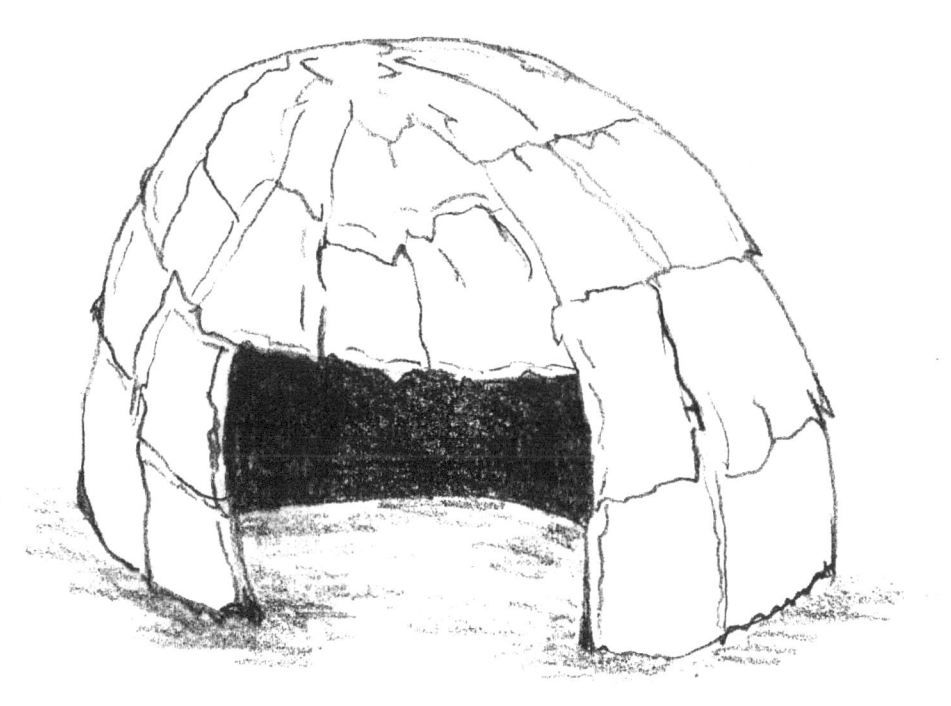

The guide quickly built a hut nice and round,
from tree bark and sticks found on the ground.
Mark's beautiful drawings were truly his pride.
Sheltered by the hut, they stayed safe and dry!

The trip could have been an adventurous flop,
save for their survival skills top-notch!
See the hatchet for chopping wood,
a pipe and a fishing spear
a bow and a quiver with arrows
and trading beads so dear.

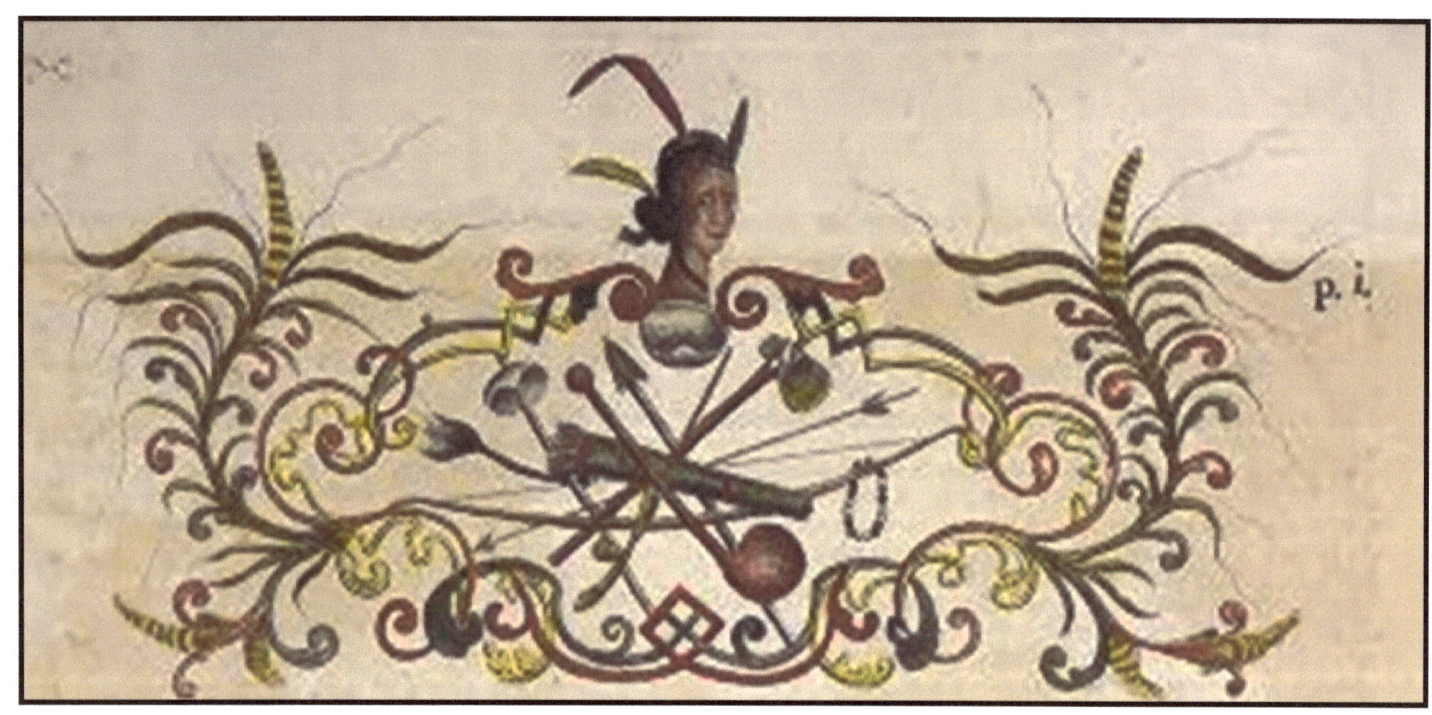

If you come to the forest, you may see me fly
from tree branch to tree branch I glide by.

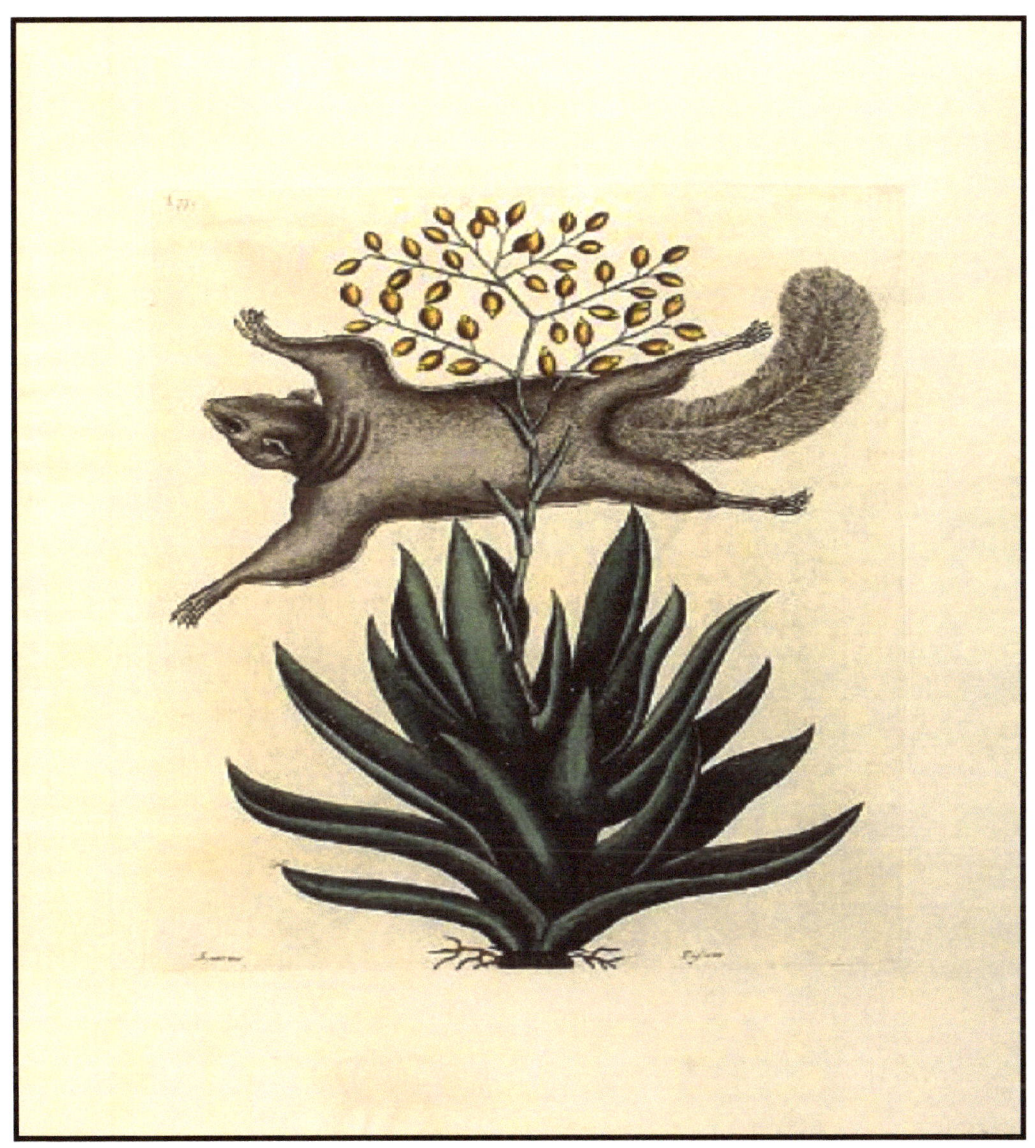

More animals and birds are drawn here--you'll see!
Let's start coloring with Mark Catesby!

Your Friend,

Flying Squirrel

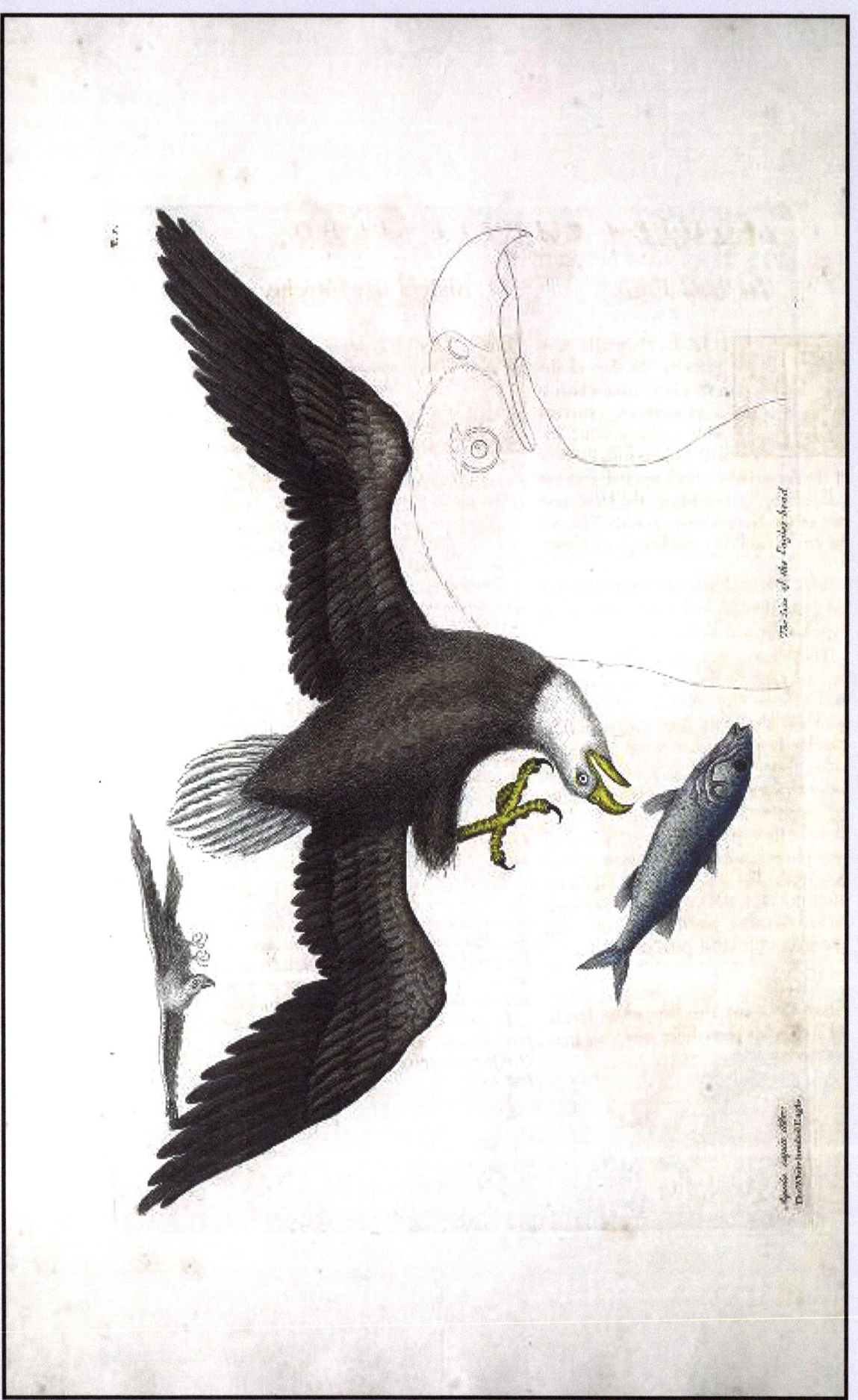

Bald Eagle

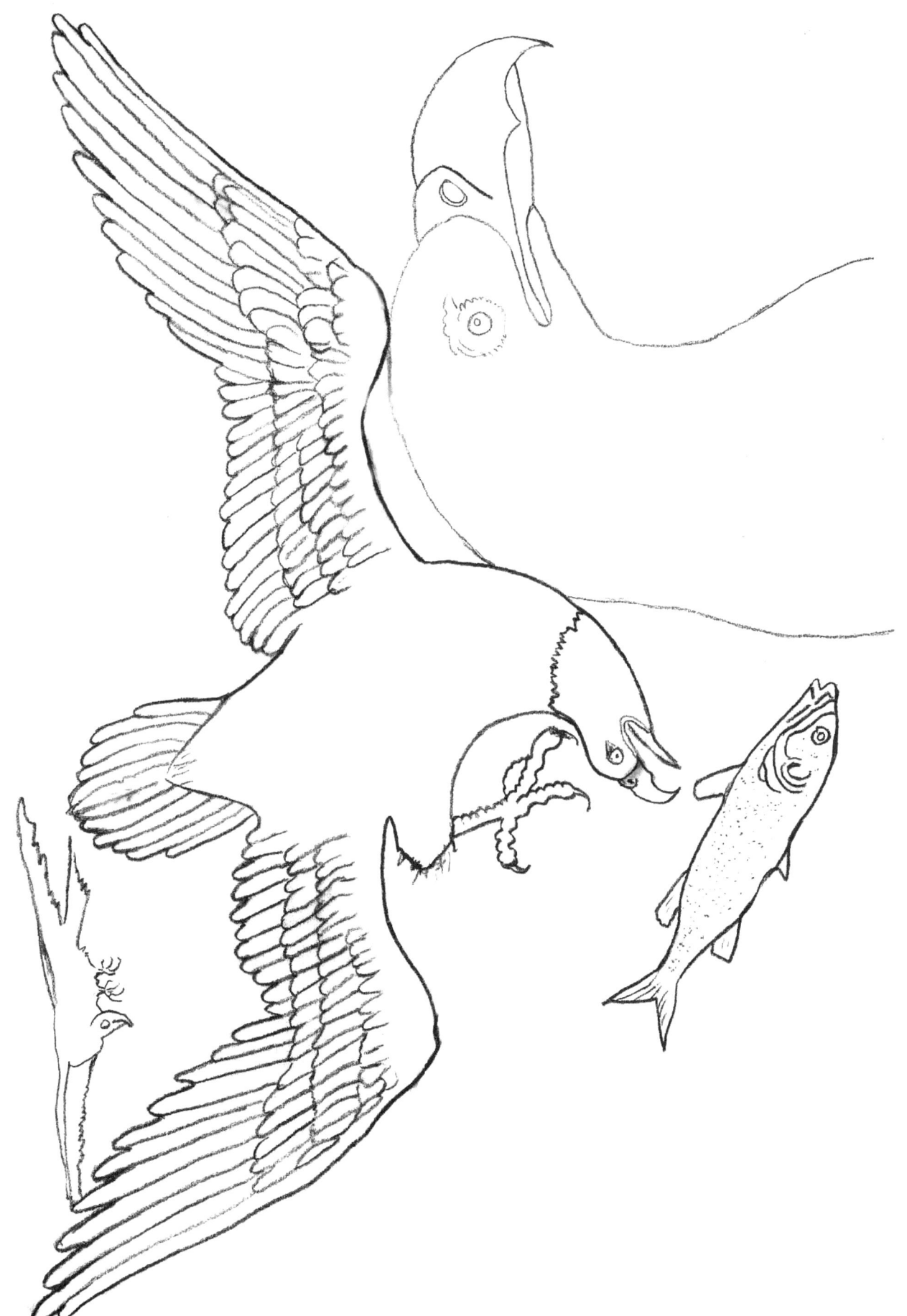

Red Winged Blackbird

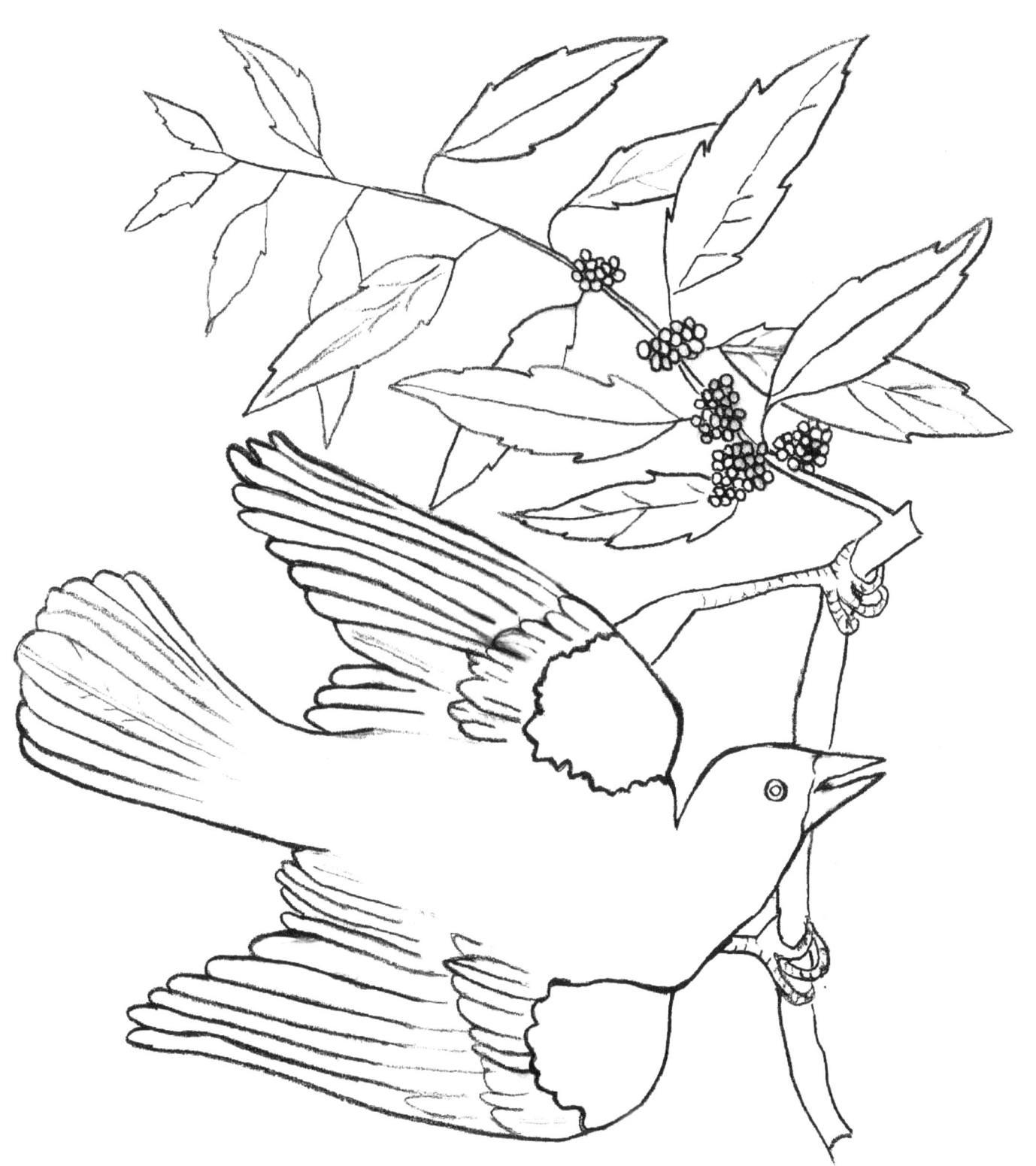

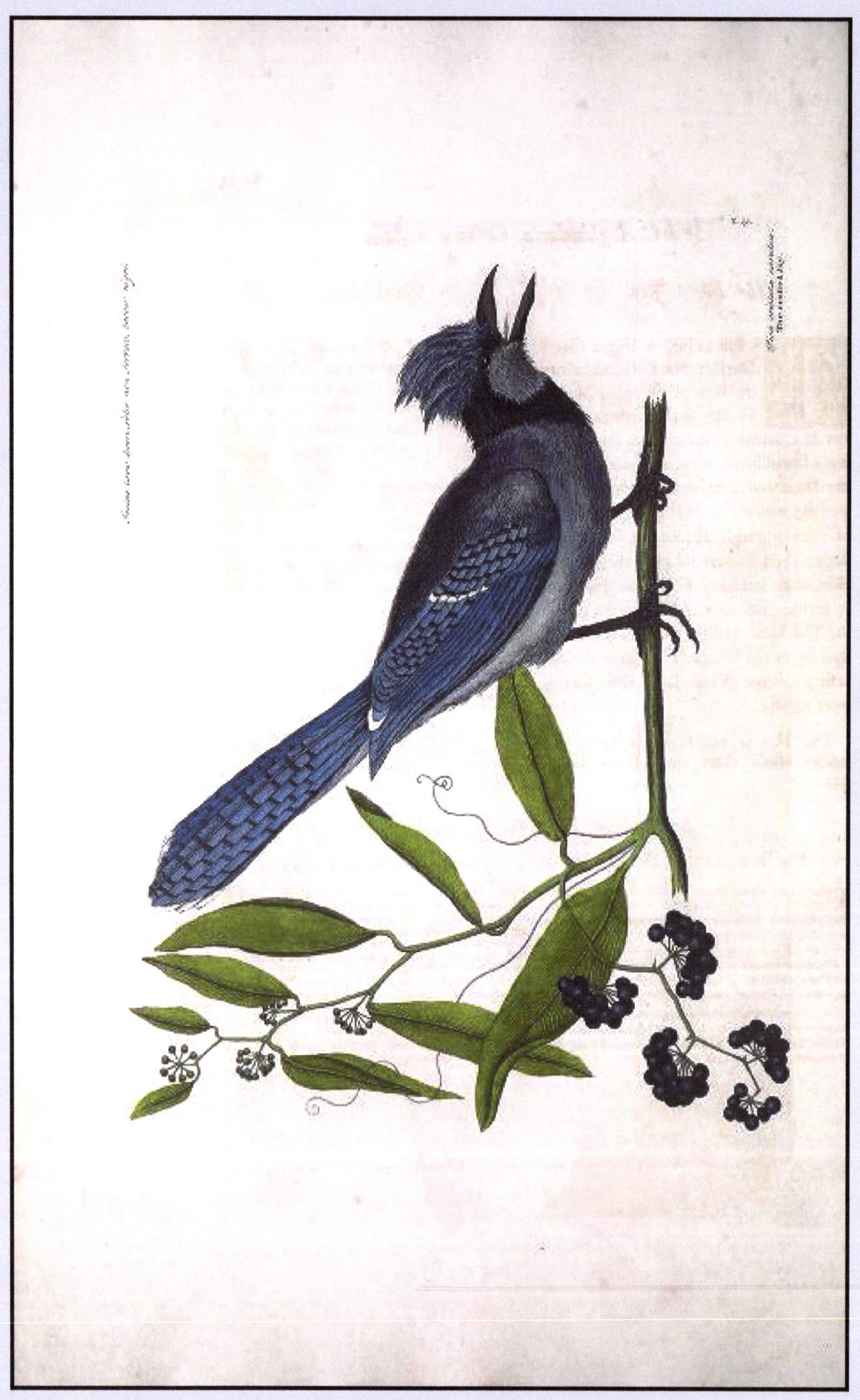

Bluejay

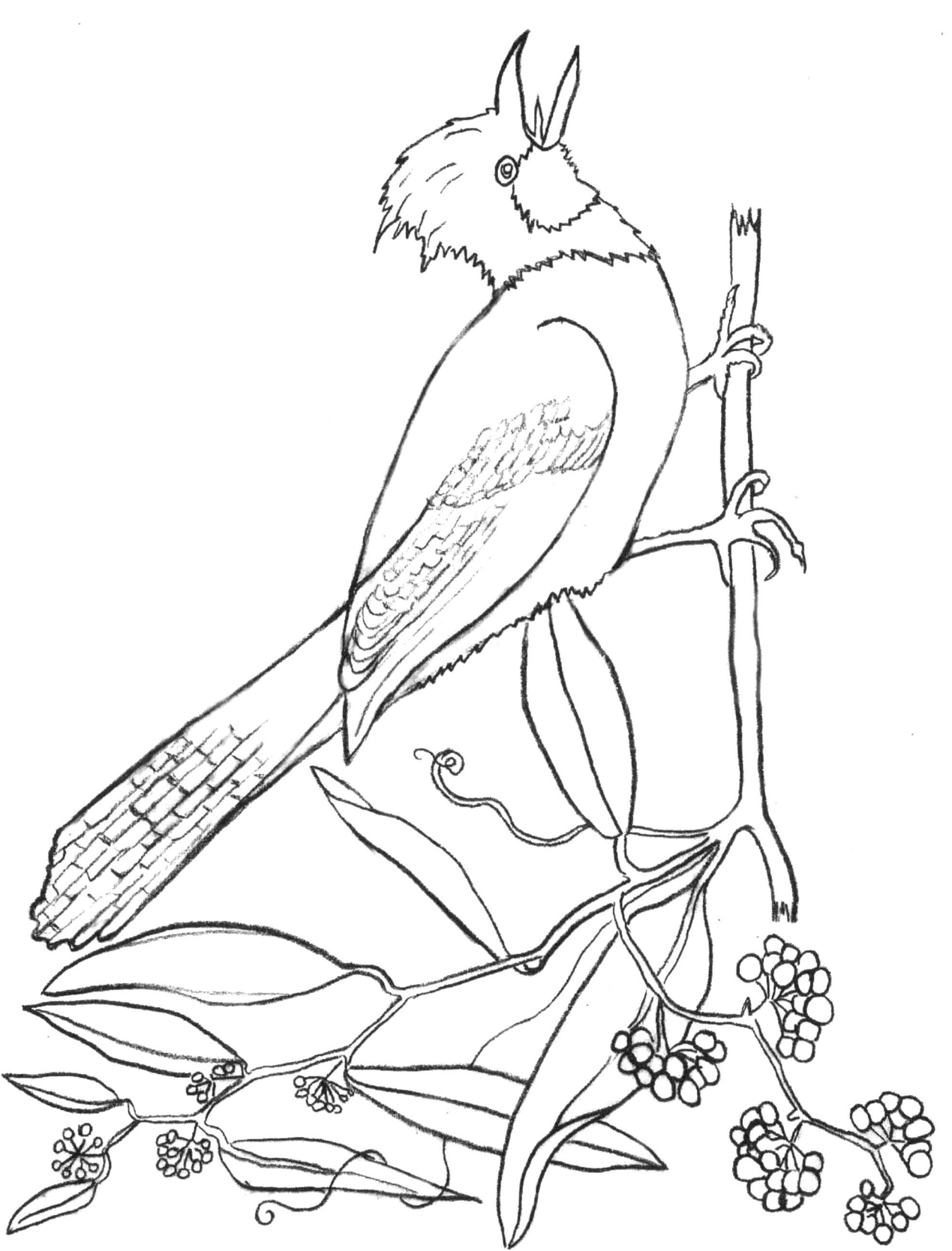

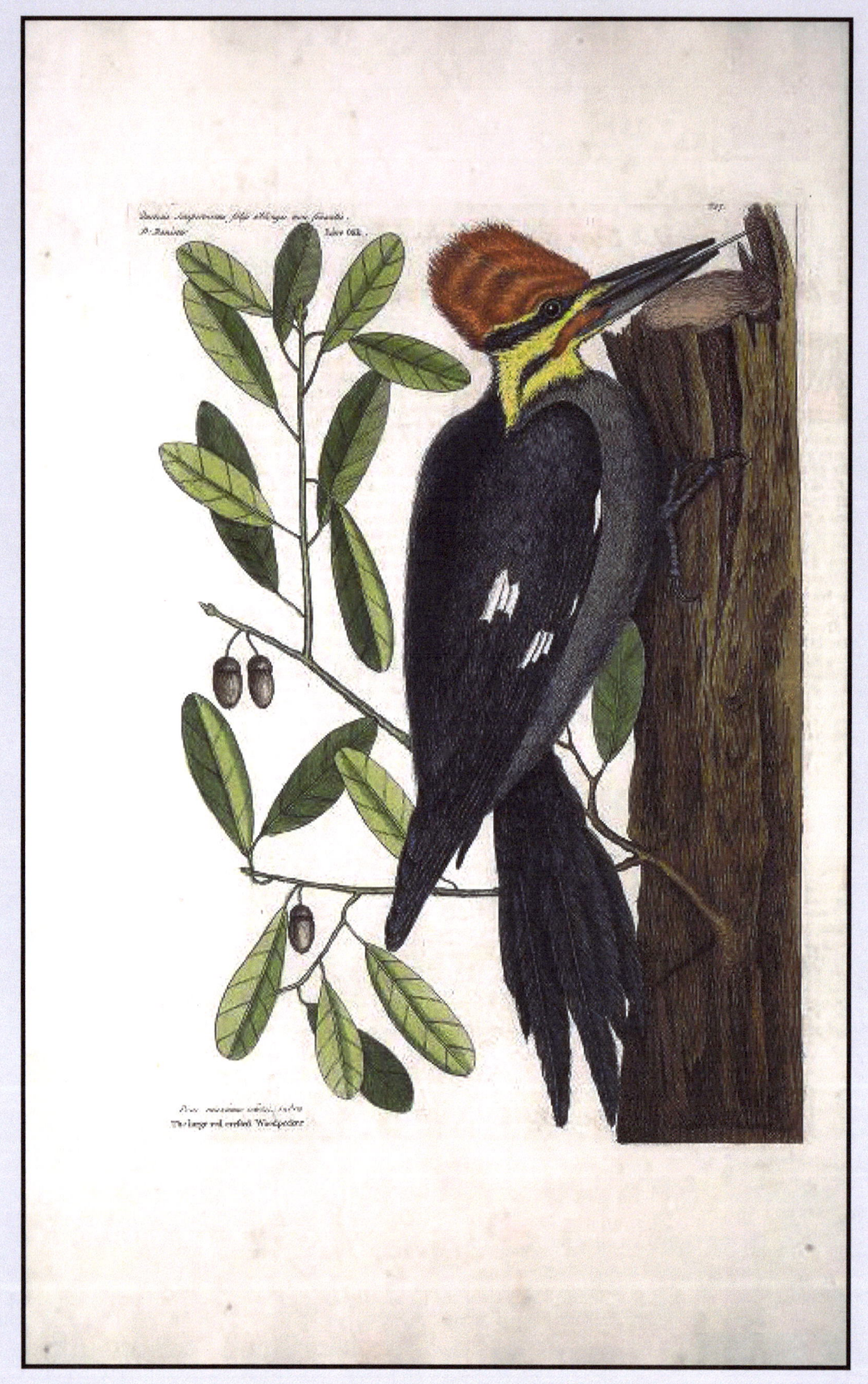

Pileated Woodpecker

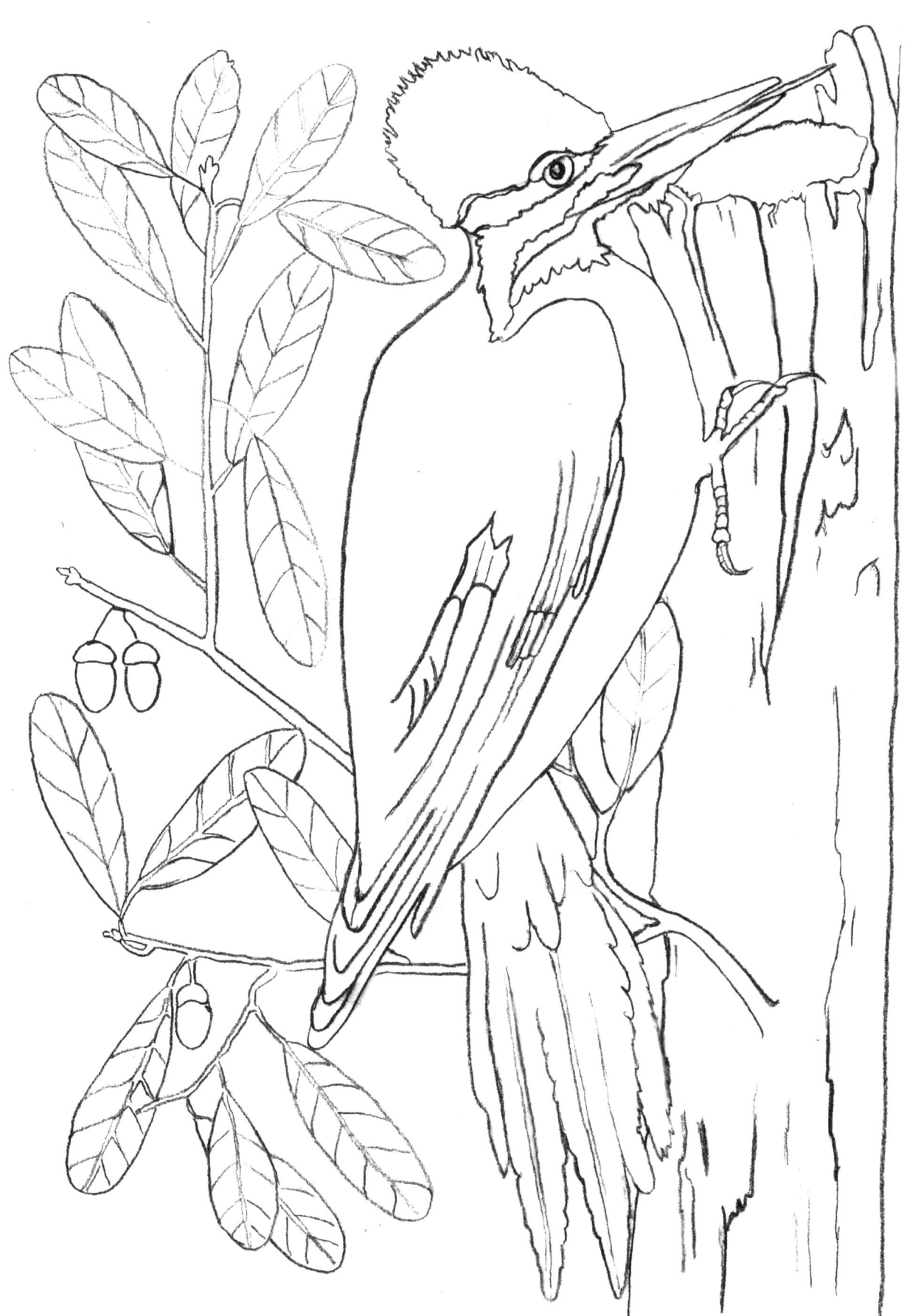

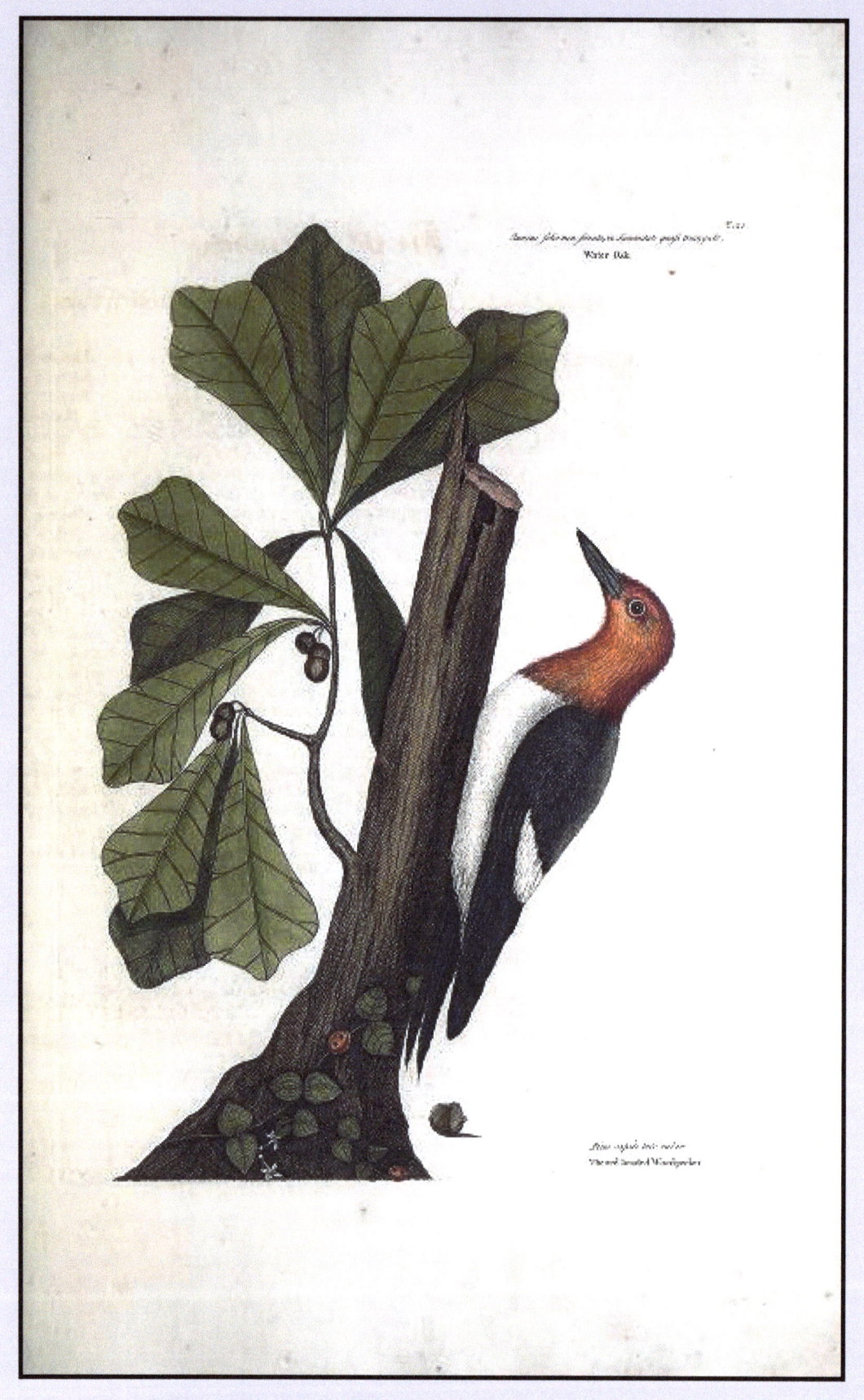

Quercus folio non serrato, foliis alongatis. P.21
Water Oak

Picus capite toto rubro
The red headed Woodpecker

Red Headed Woodpecker

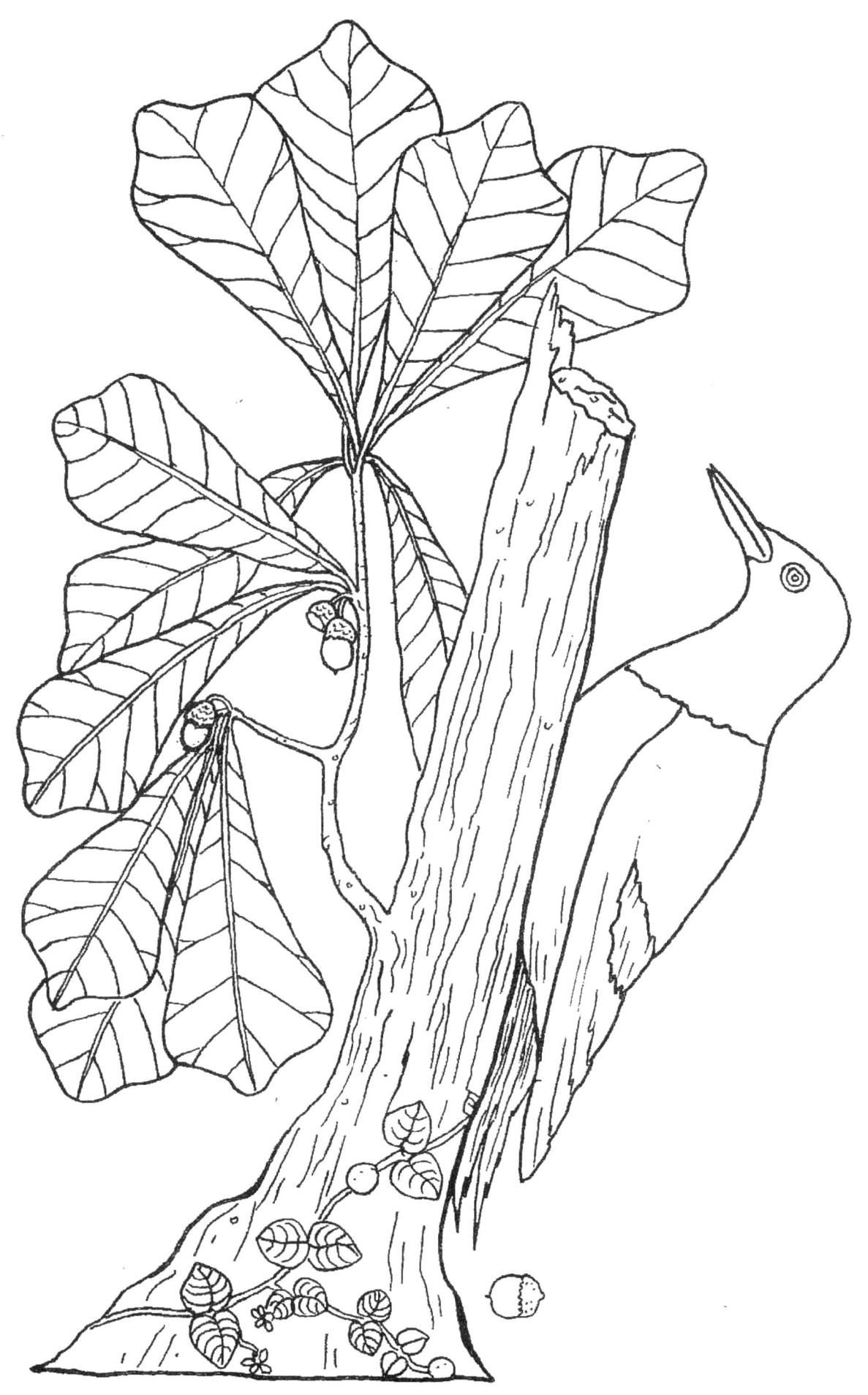

Courtesy of Susan Smith Cavanagh

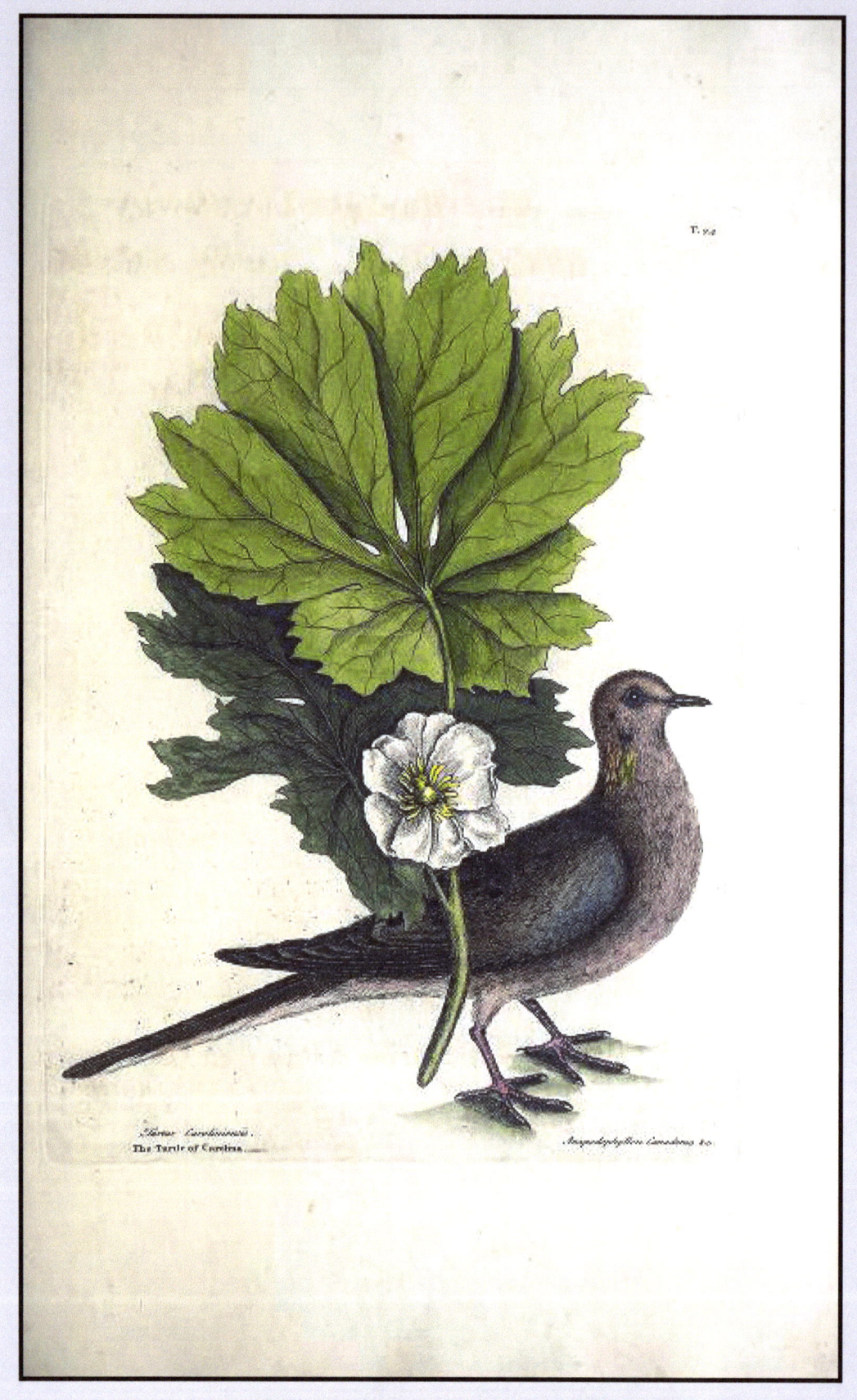

Turtur Carolinensis.
The Turtle of Carolina.

Anapodophyllon Canadense &c.

Mourning Dove

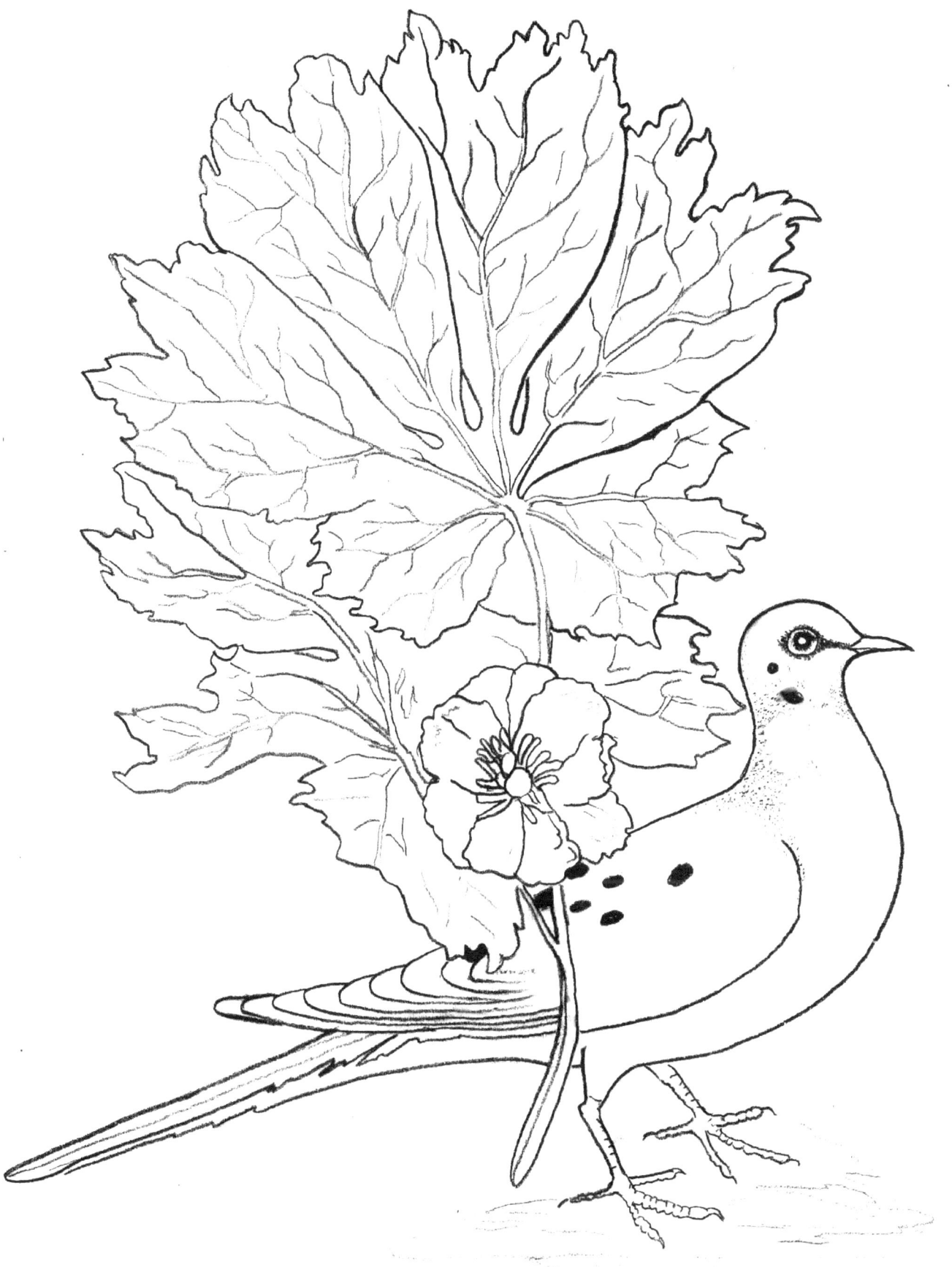

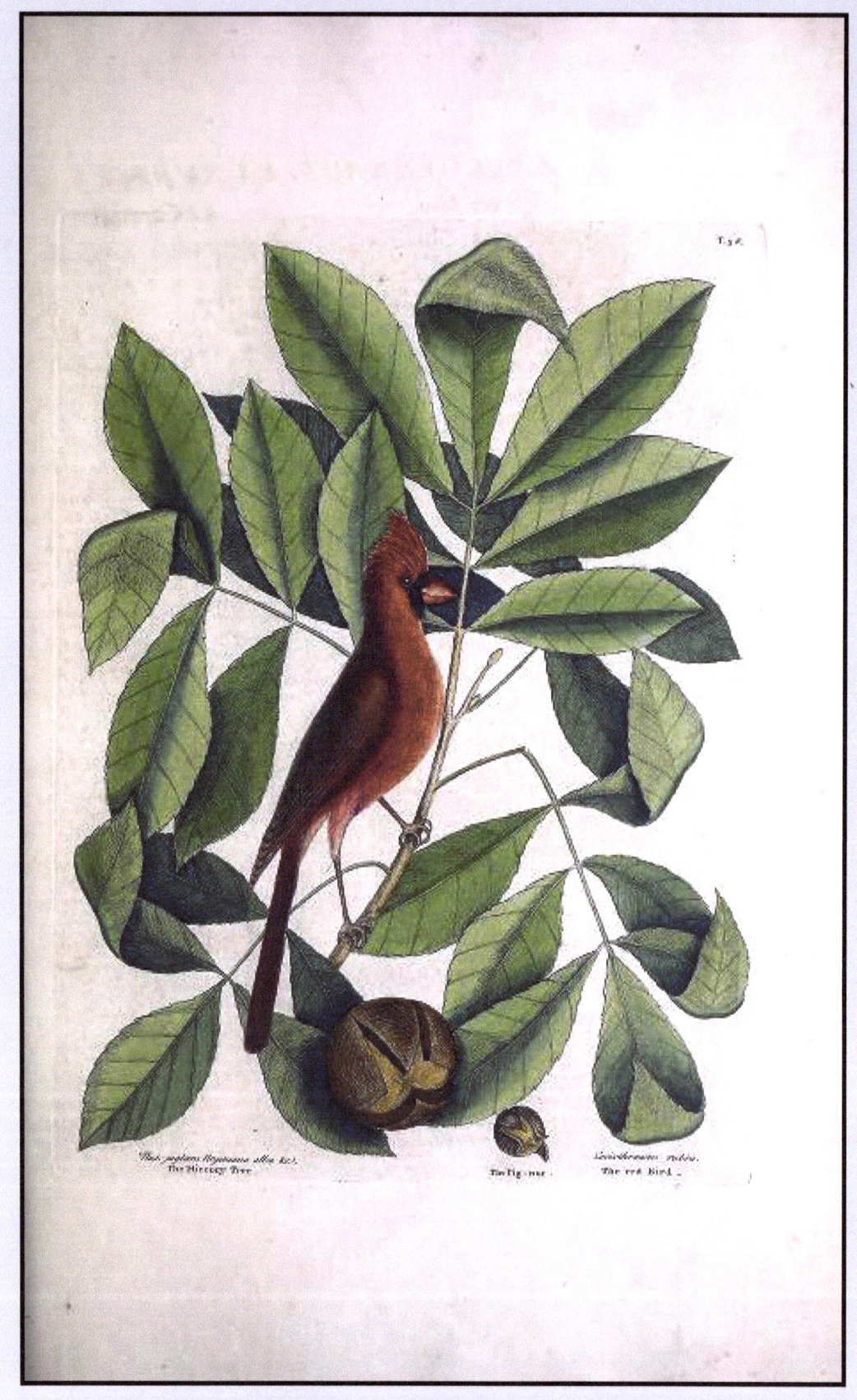

T.38.

Phus aeplens Virginiana albae &c.
The Hiccory Tree

The Fig-nut.

Loxidthornus rubro.
The red Bird.

Northern Cardinal

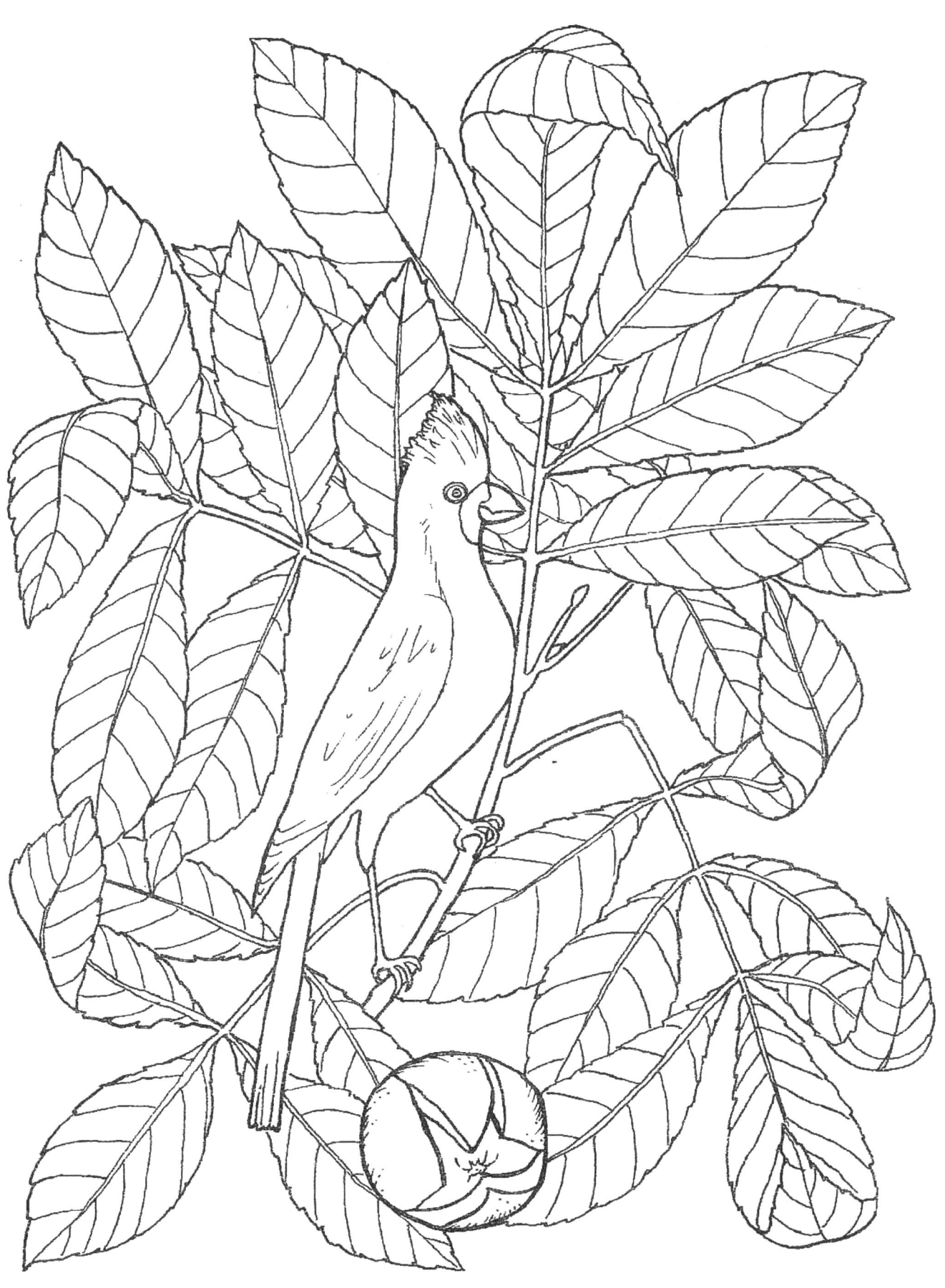

Courtesy of Susan Smith Cavanagh

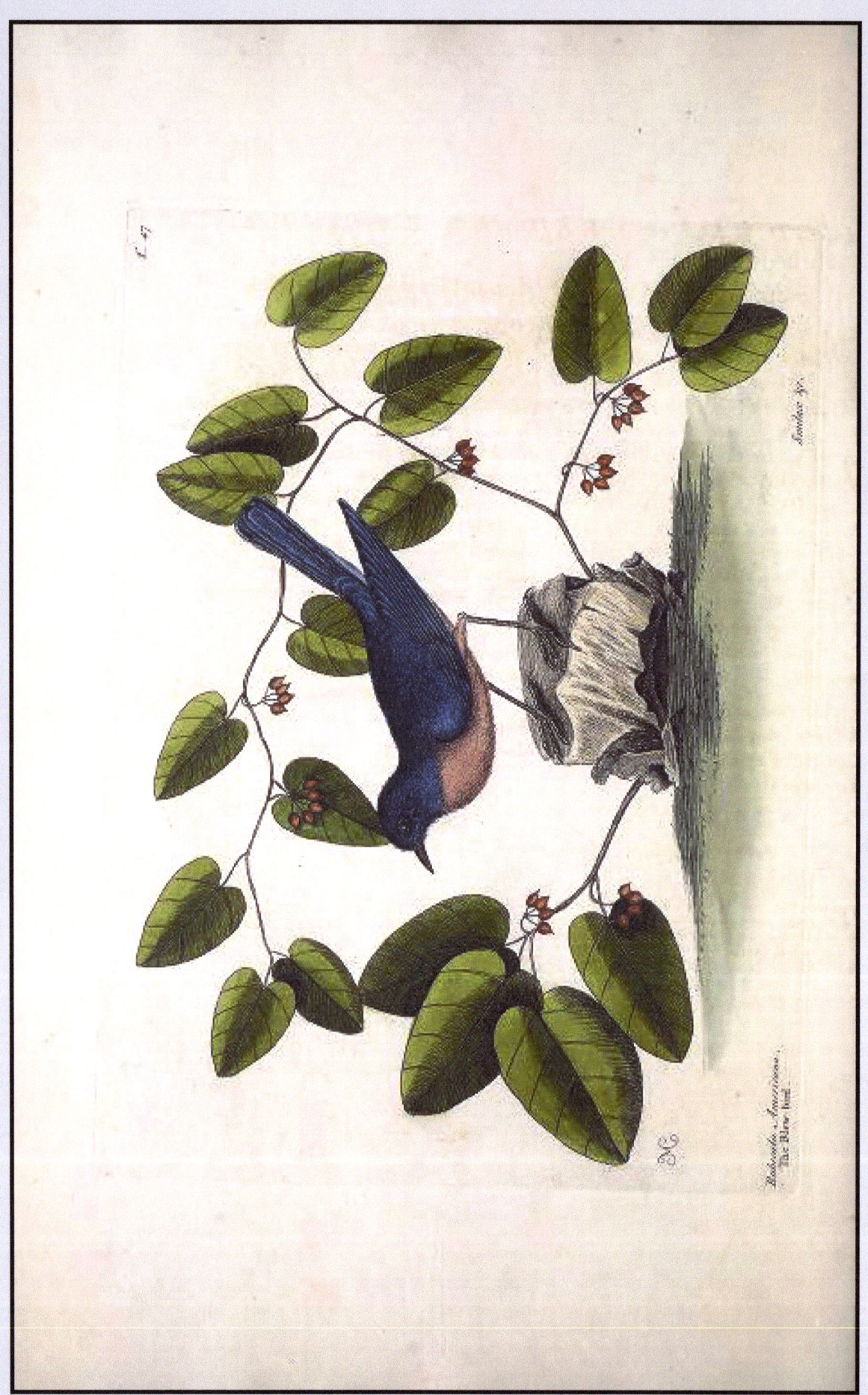

Eastern Bluebird

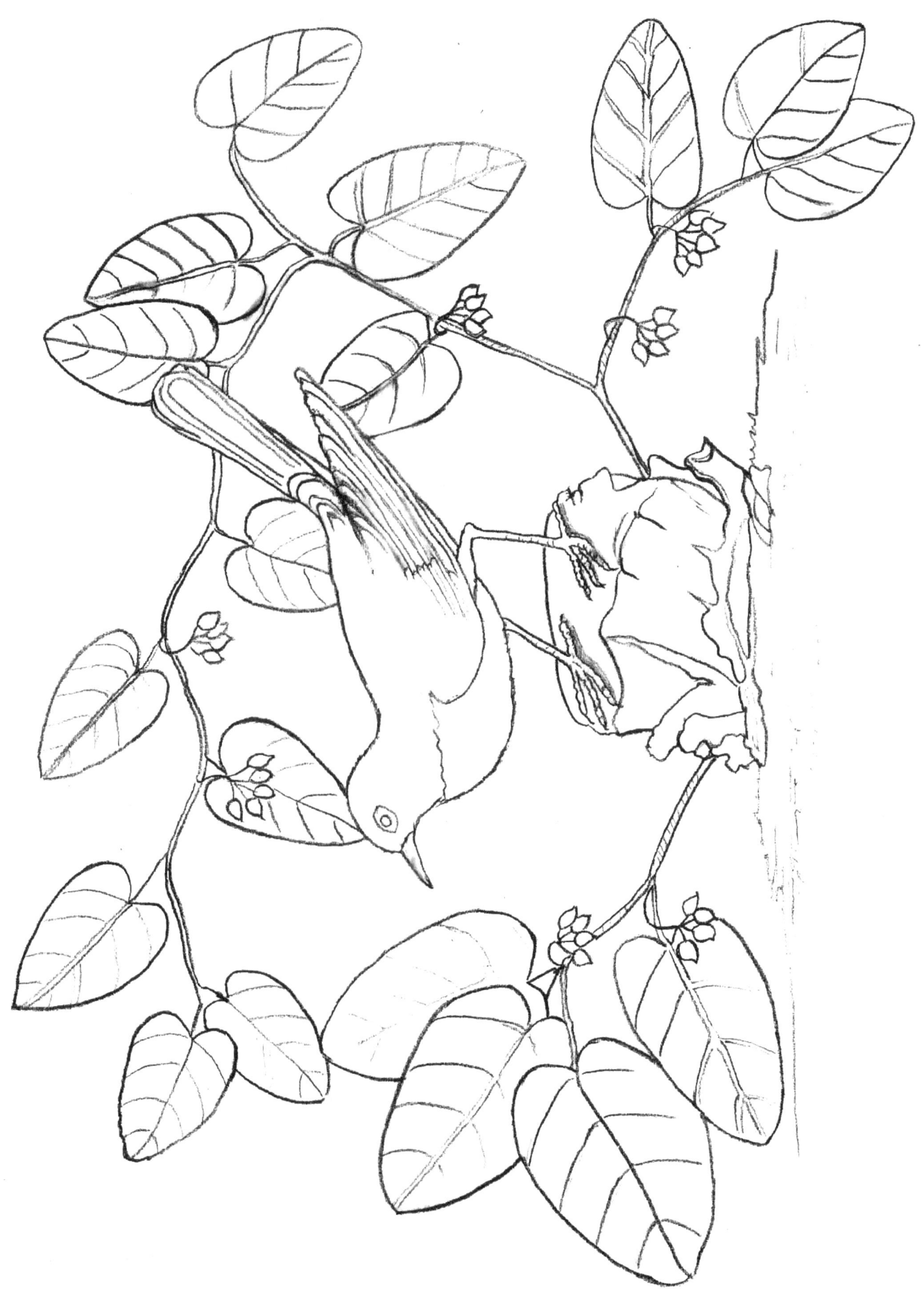

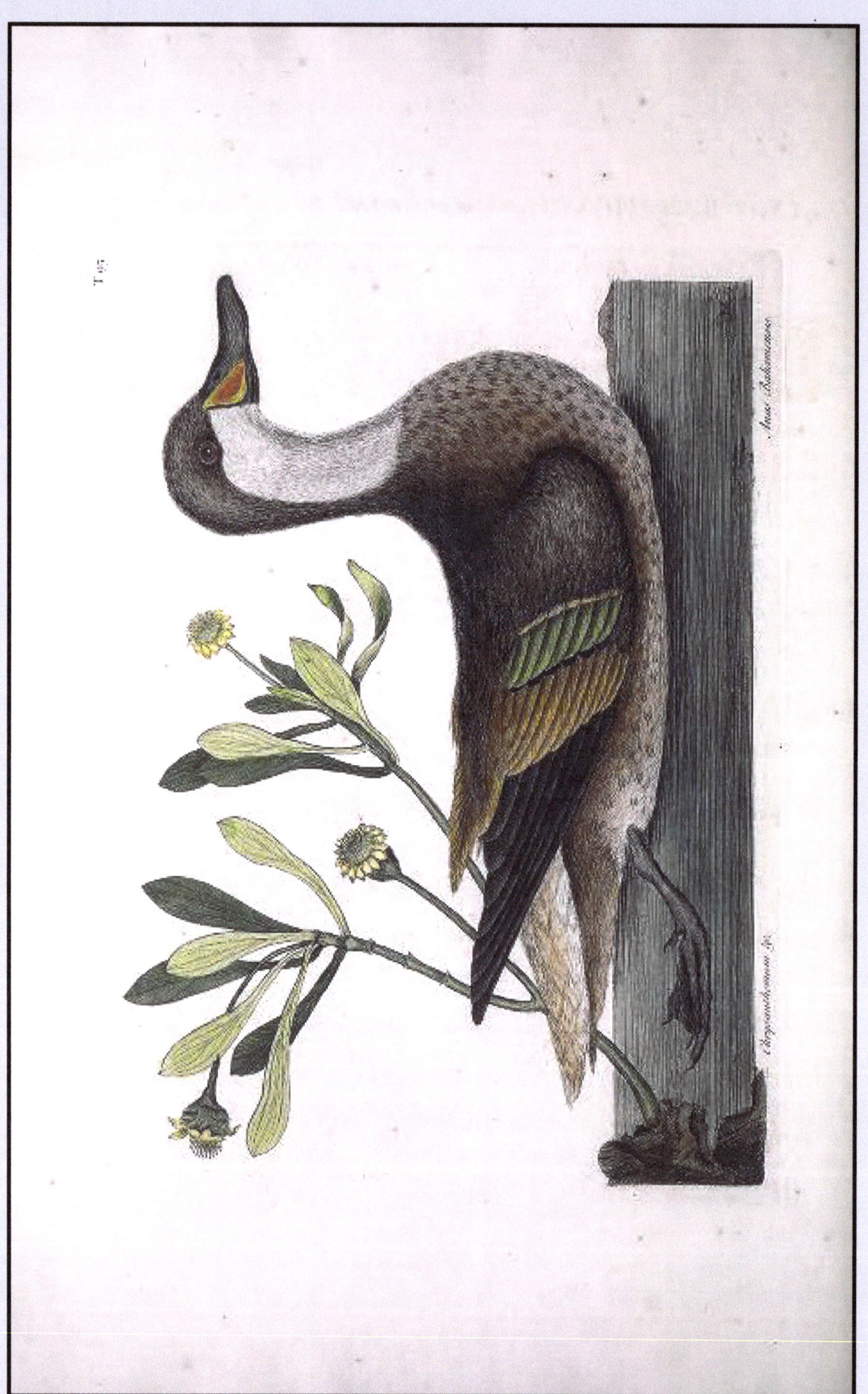

White-cheeked Pintail Duck

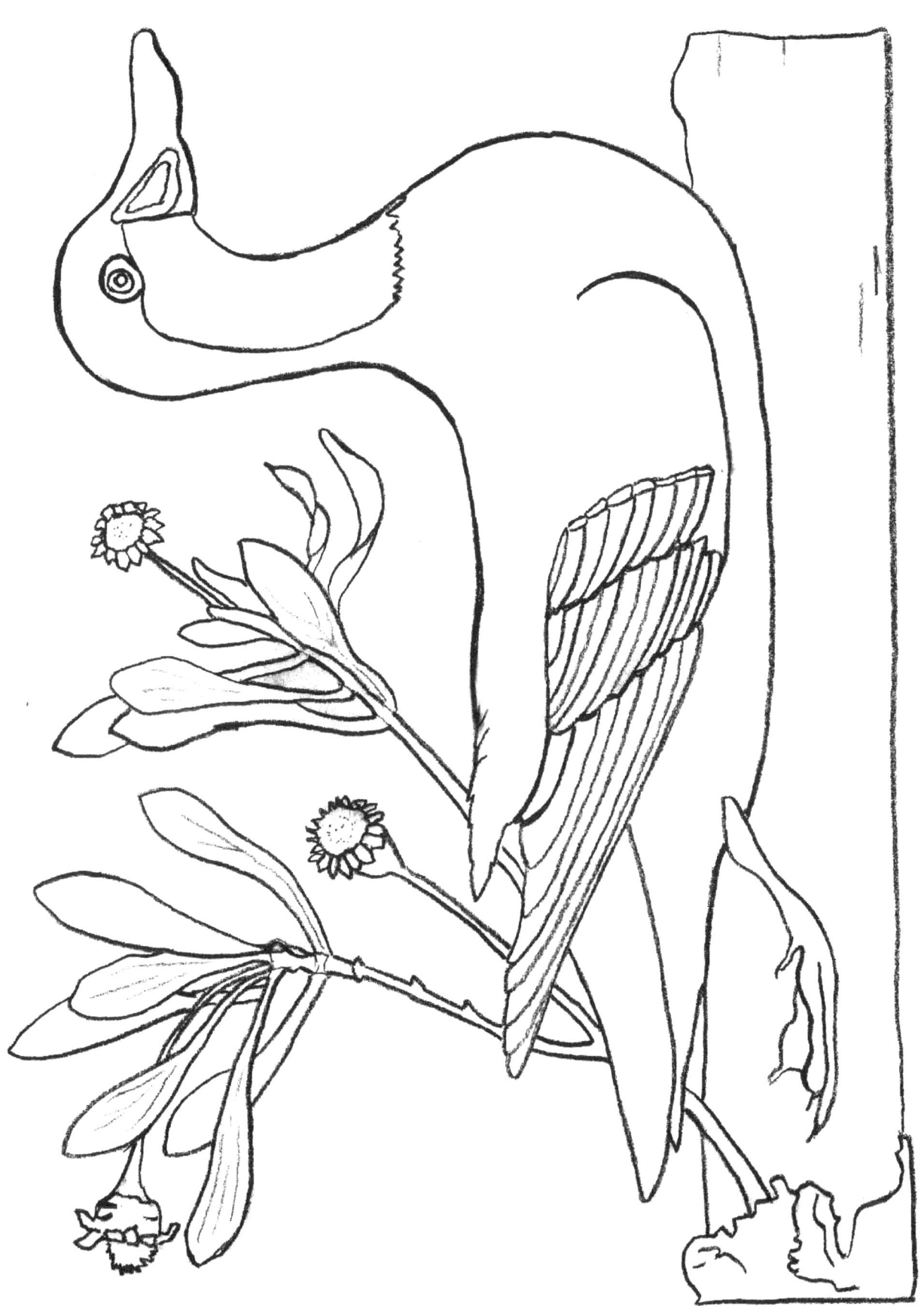

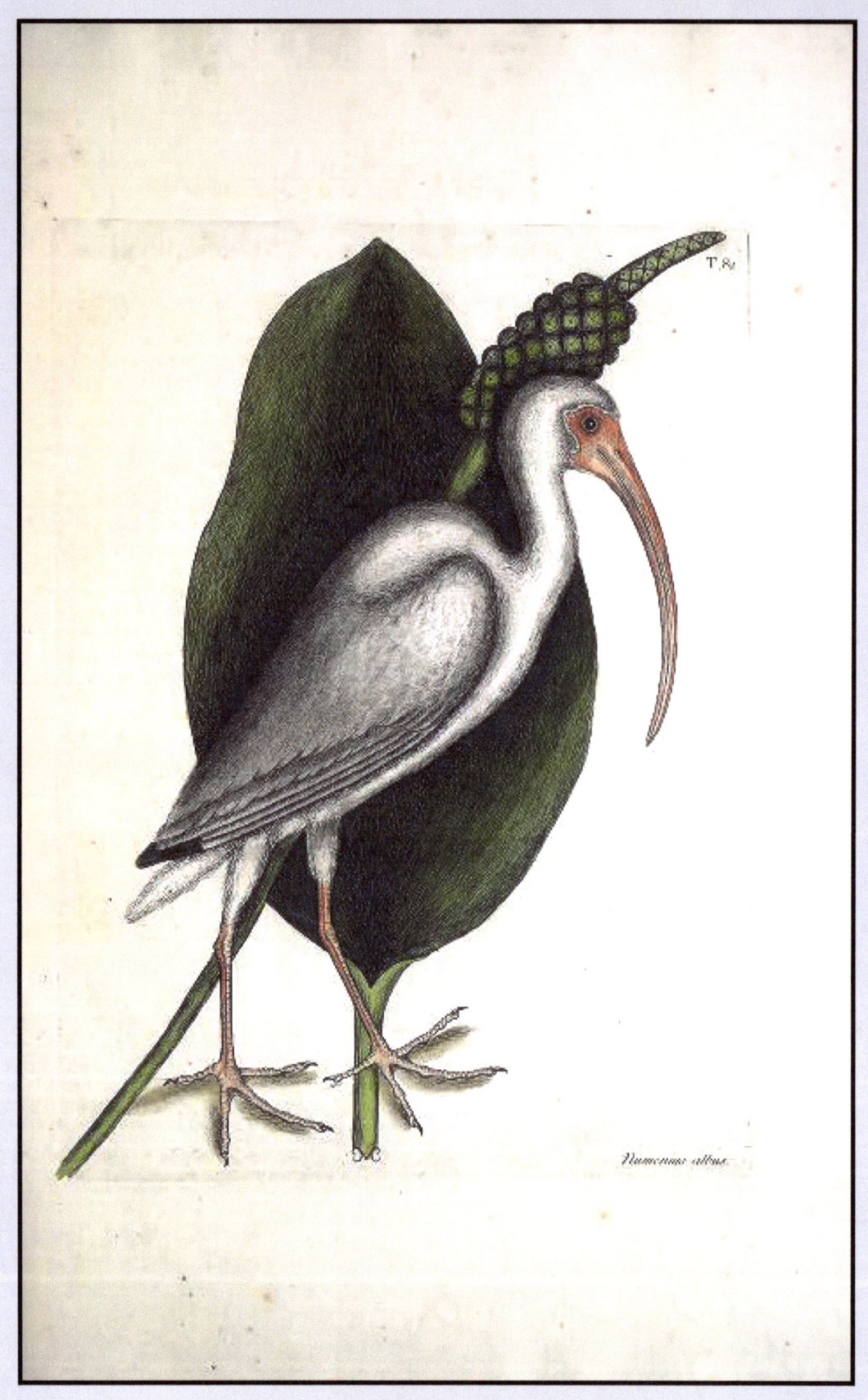

T. 82

Numenius albus.

White Ibis

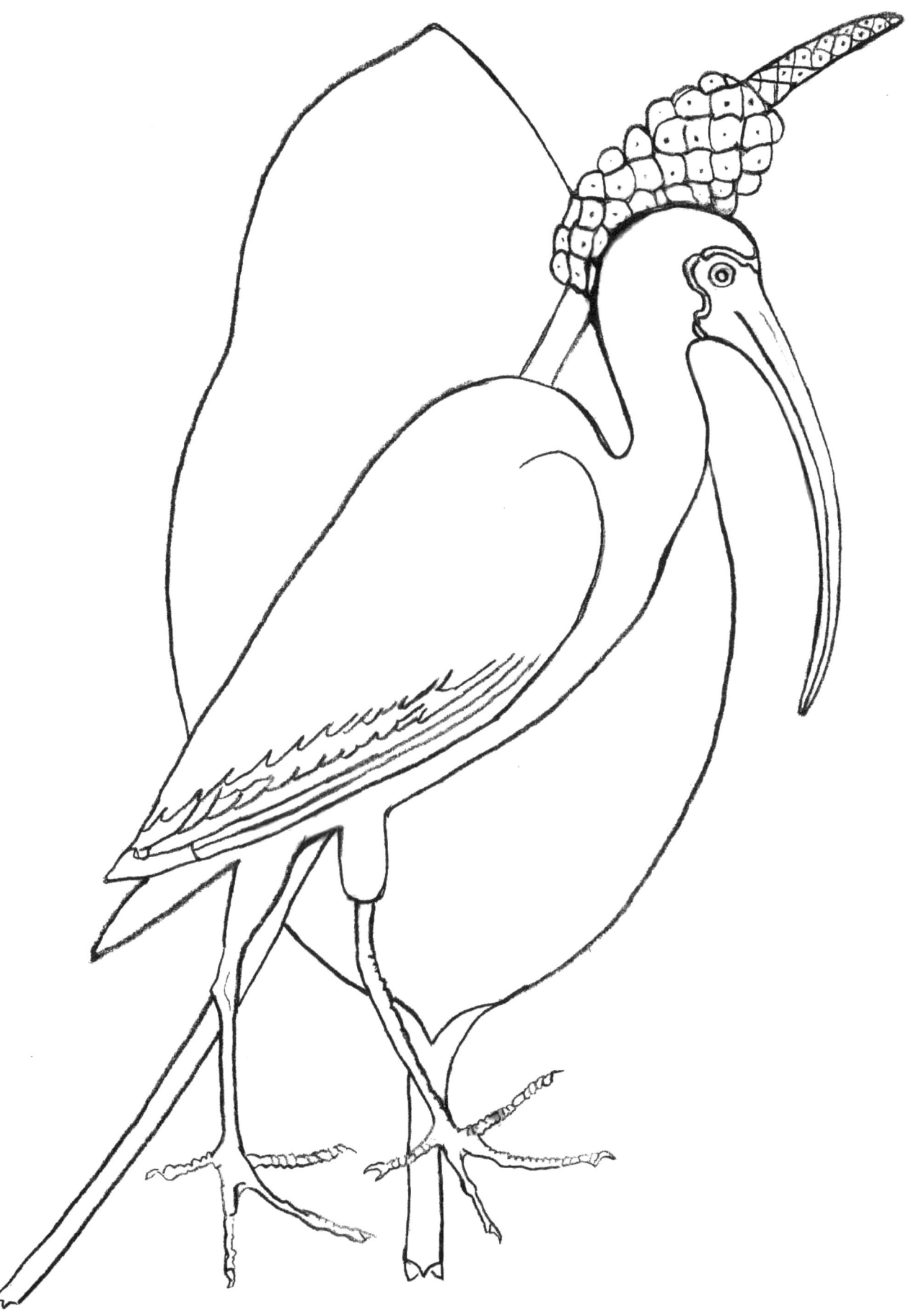

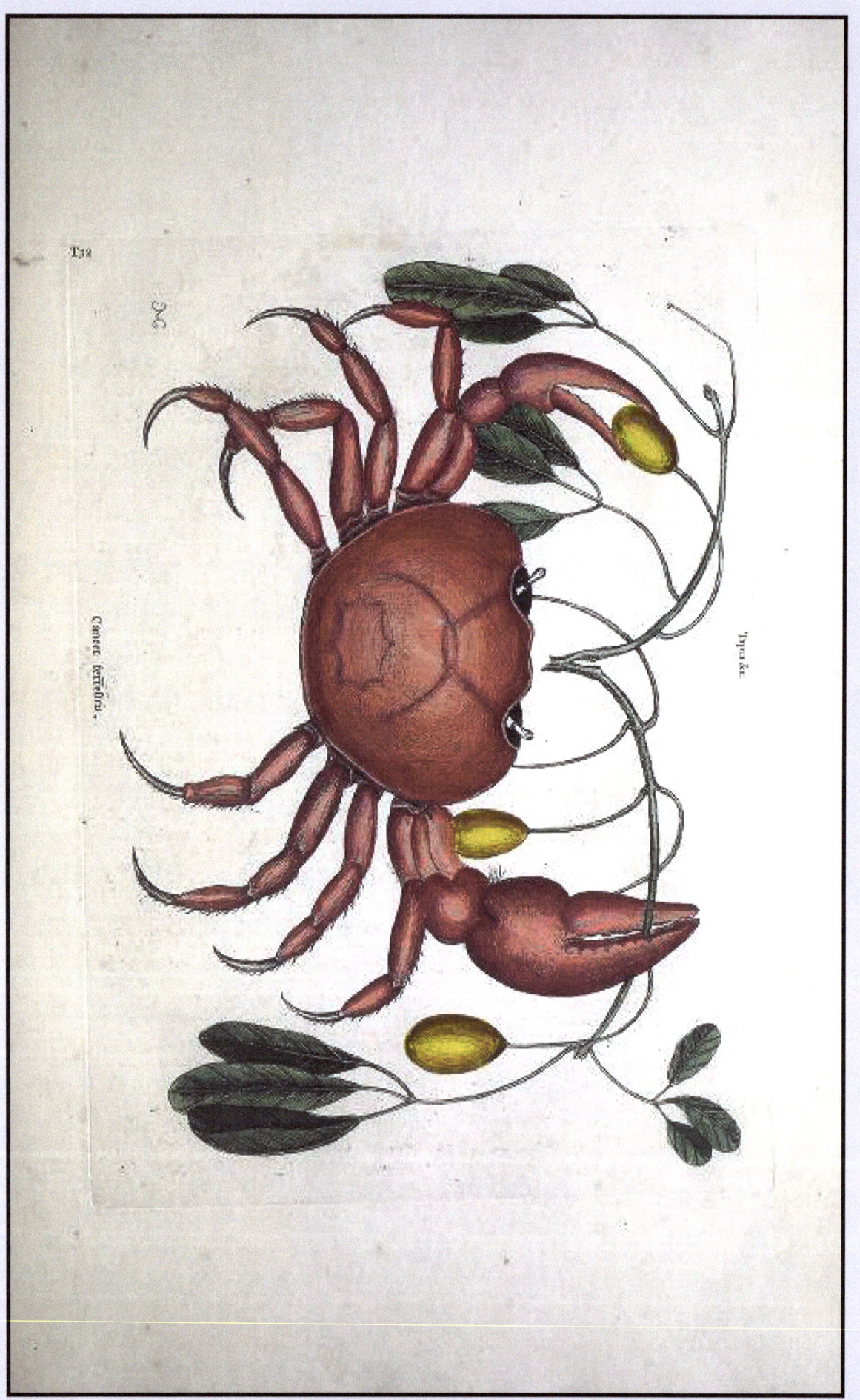

Purple Land Crab

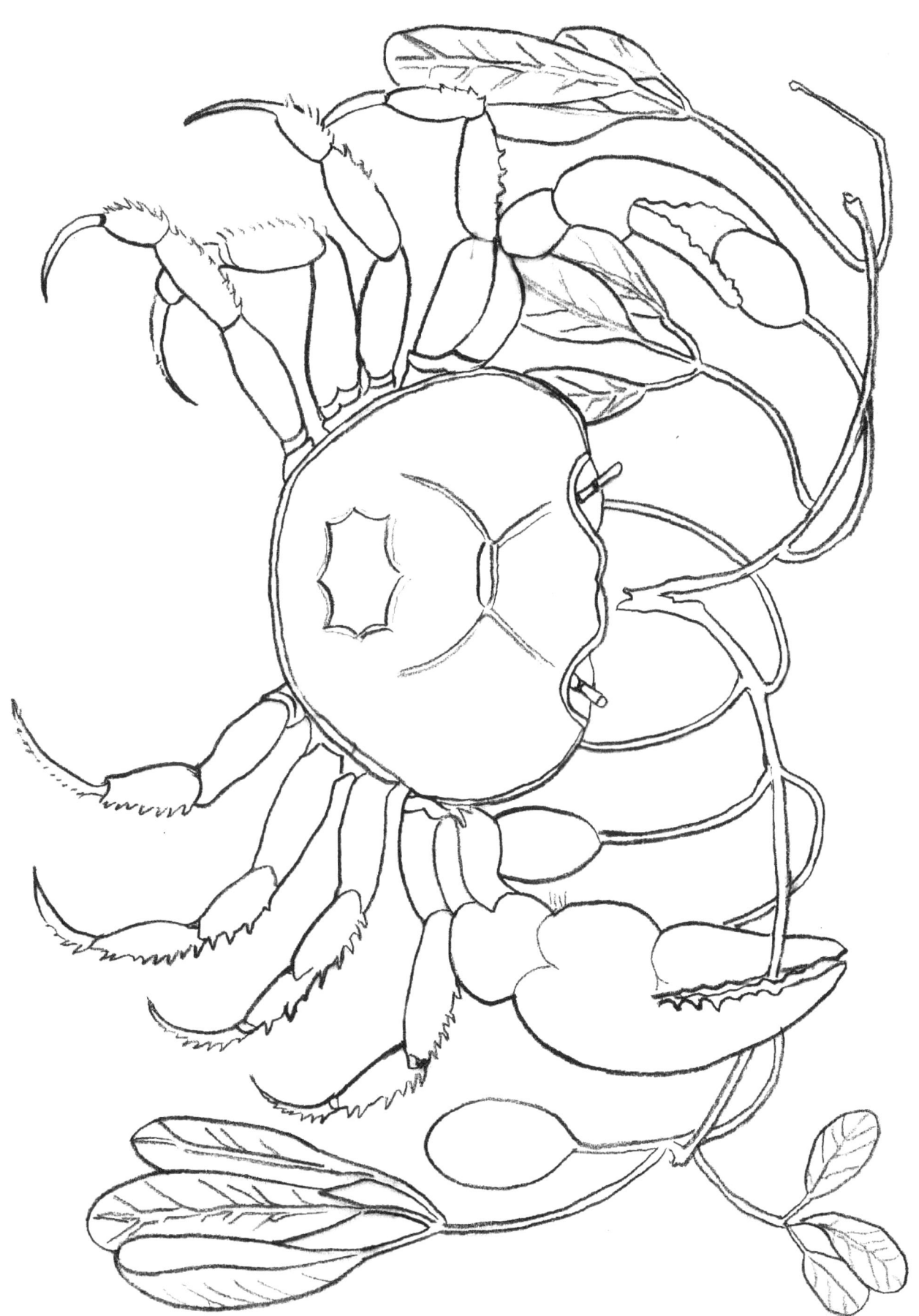

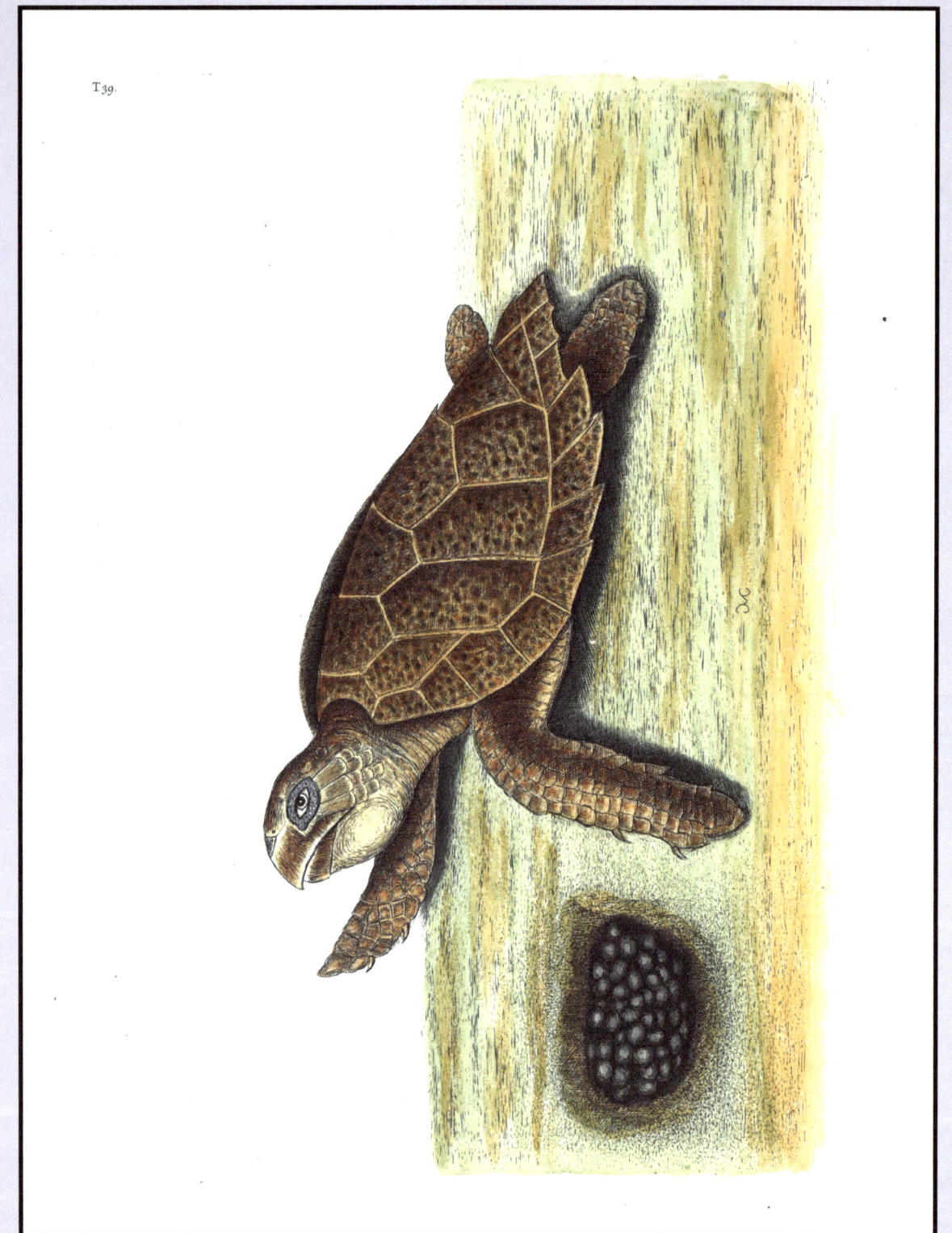

T 39.

Hawksbill Turtle

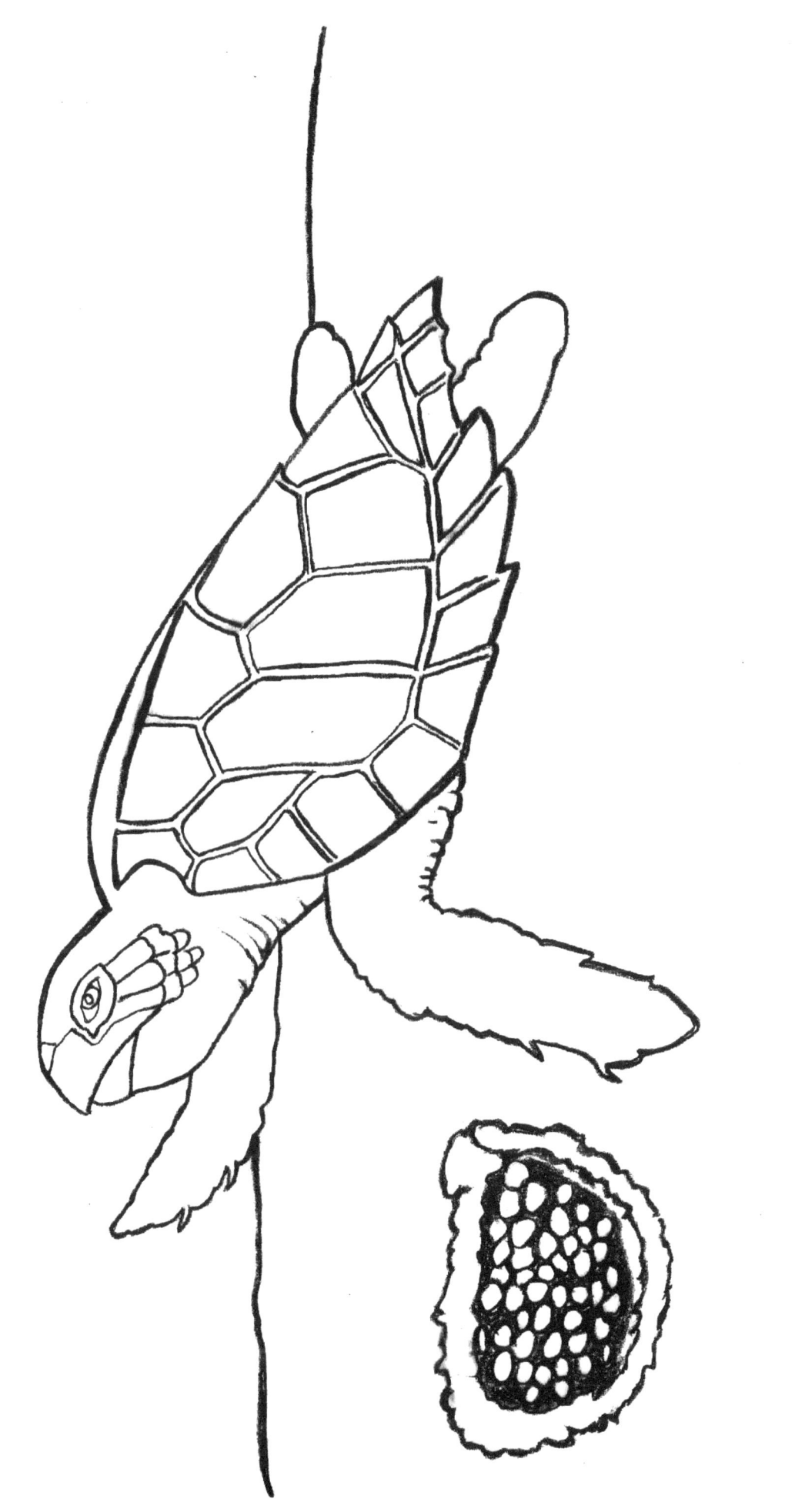

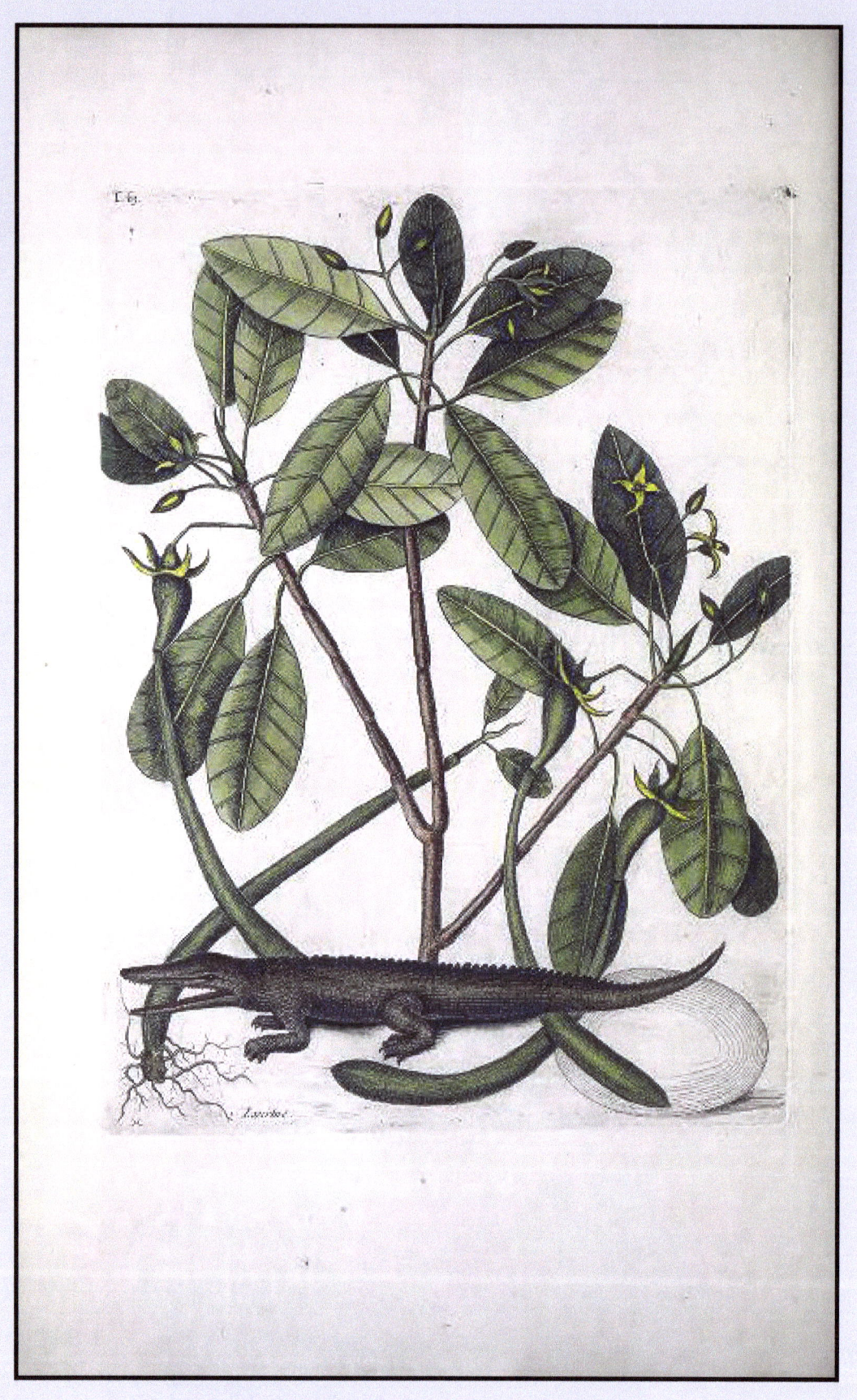

Alligator

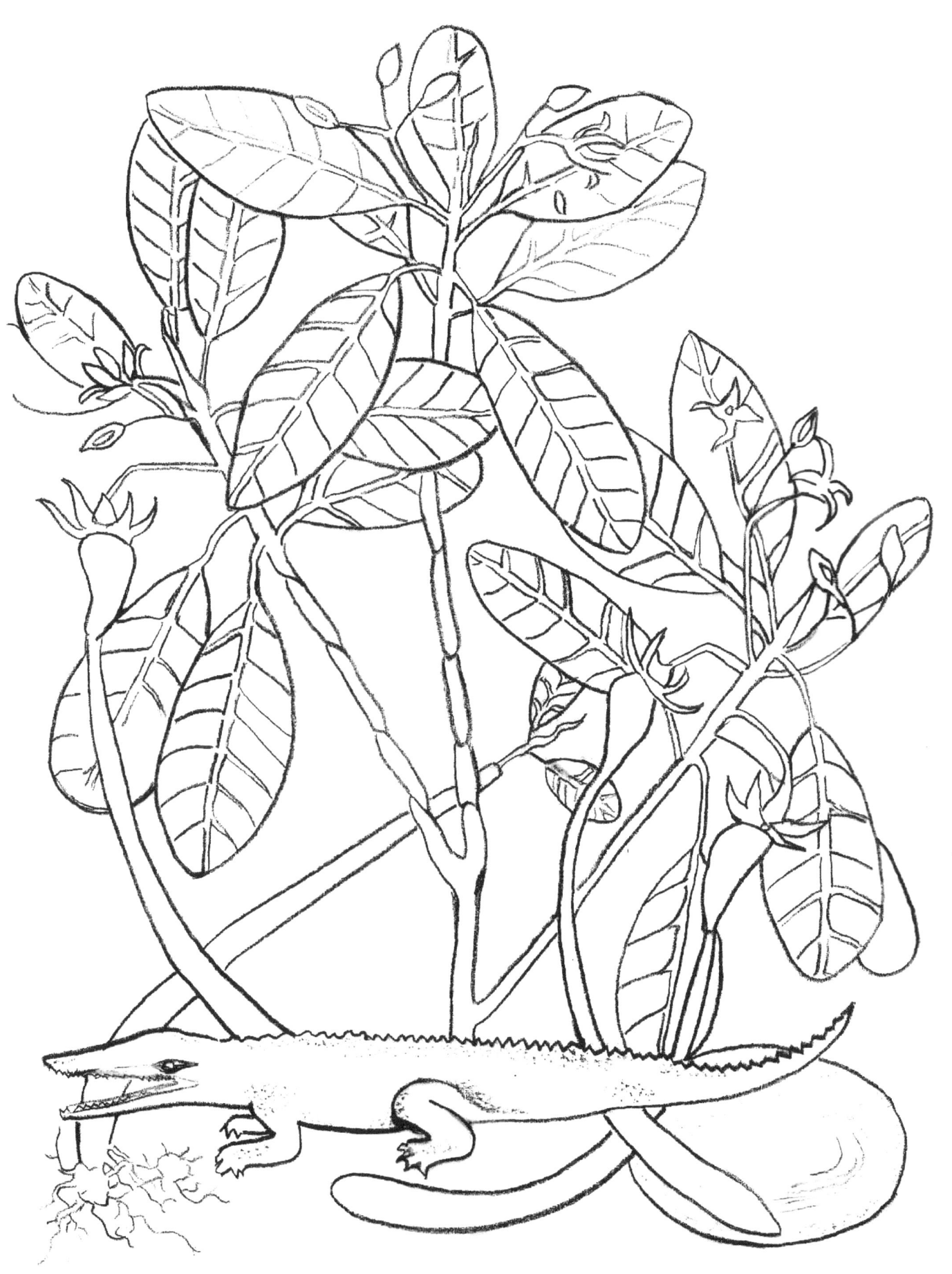

Rana maxima   Helleborens

American Bull Frog

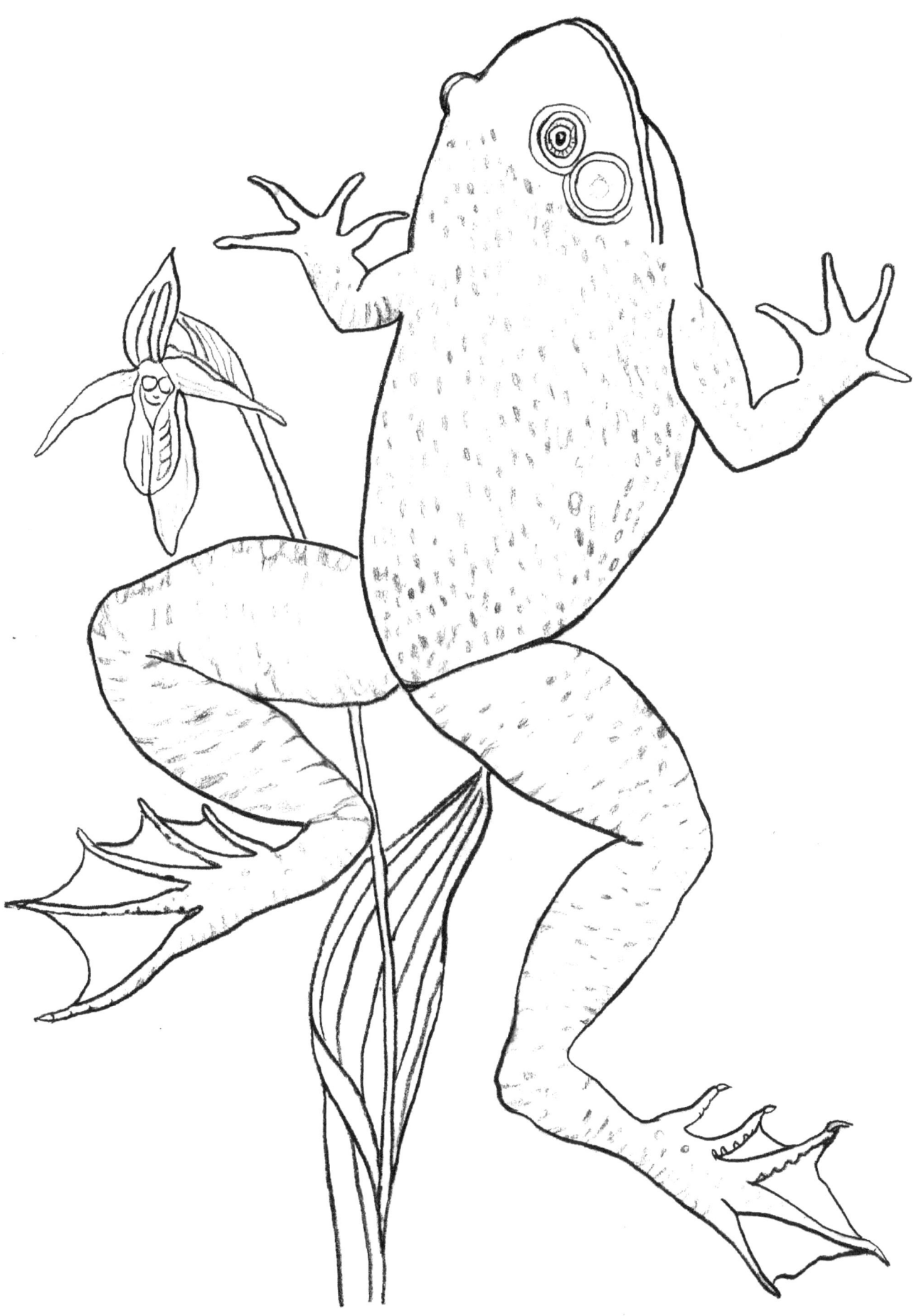

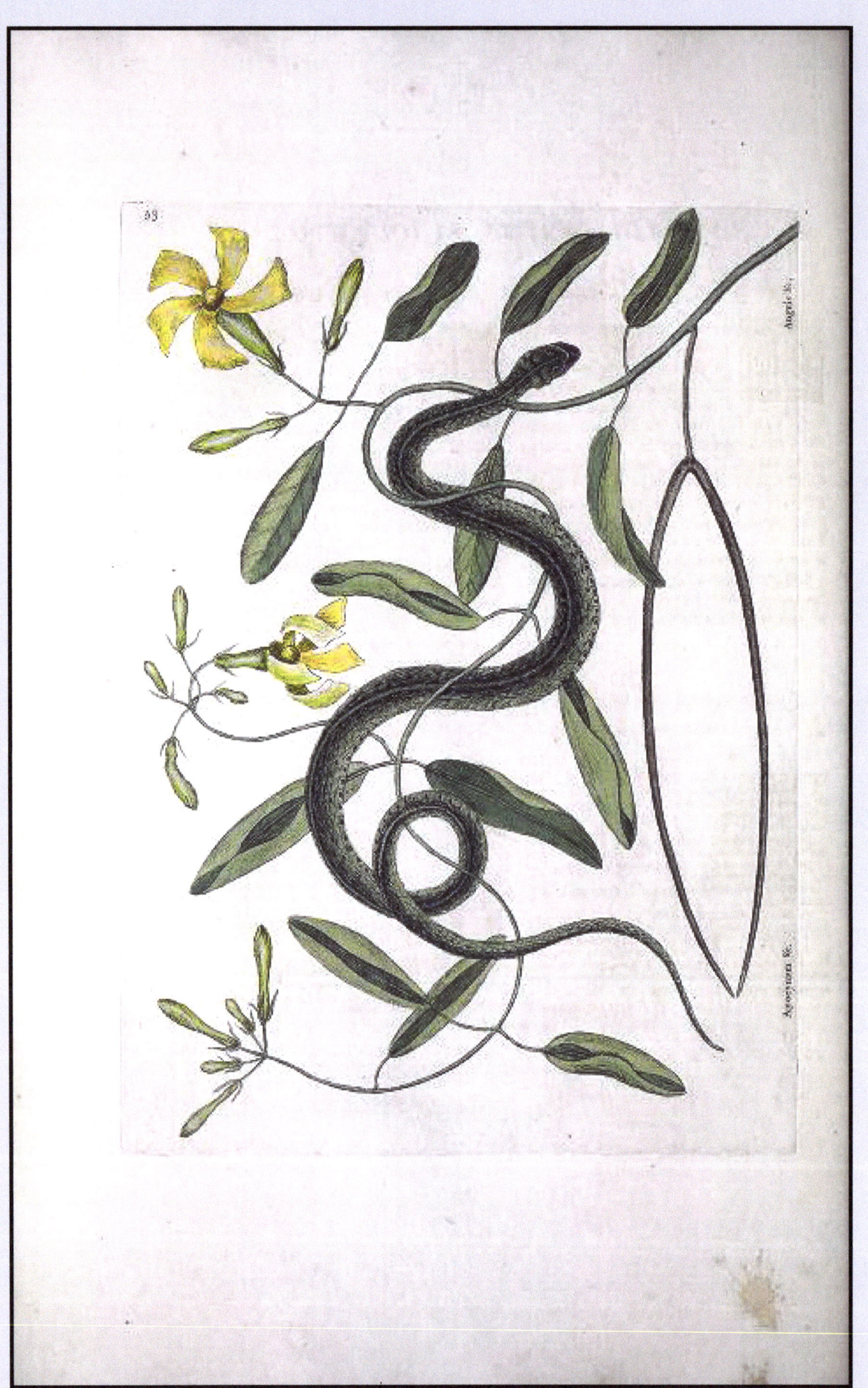

Common Garter Snake

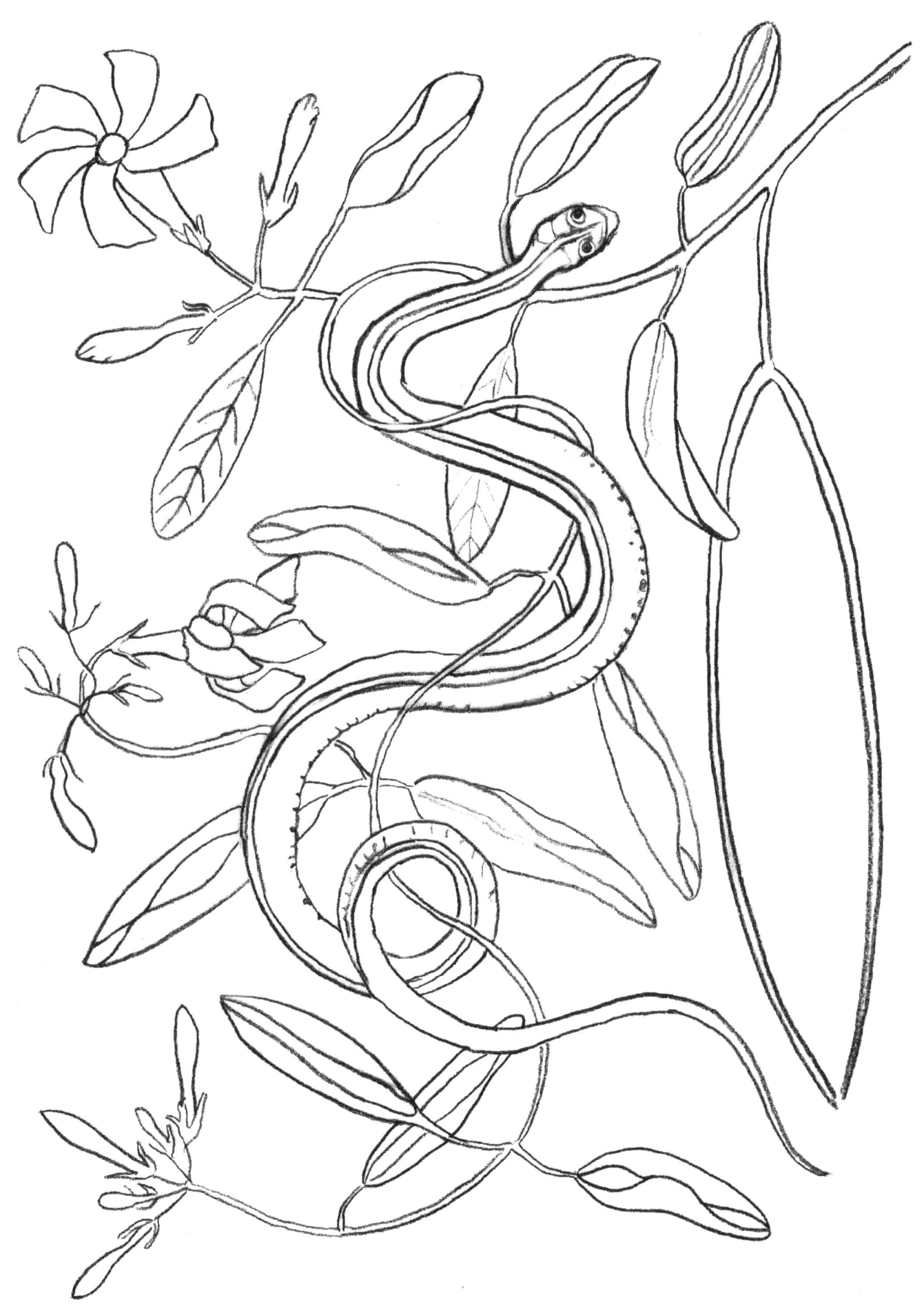

41

A Tooth.

Vipera caudisona.

The Section of a Rattle.

A Rattle of twenty-one joints.

Rattlesnake

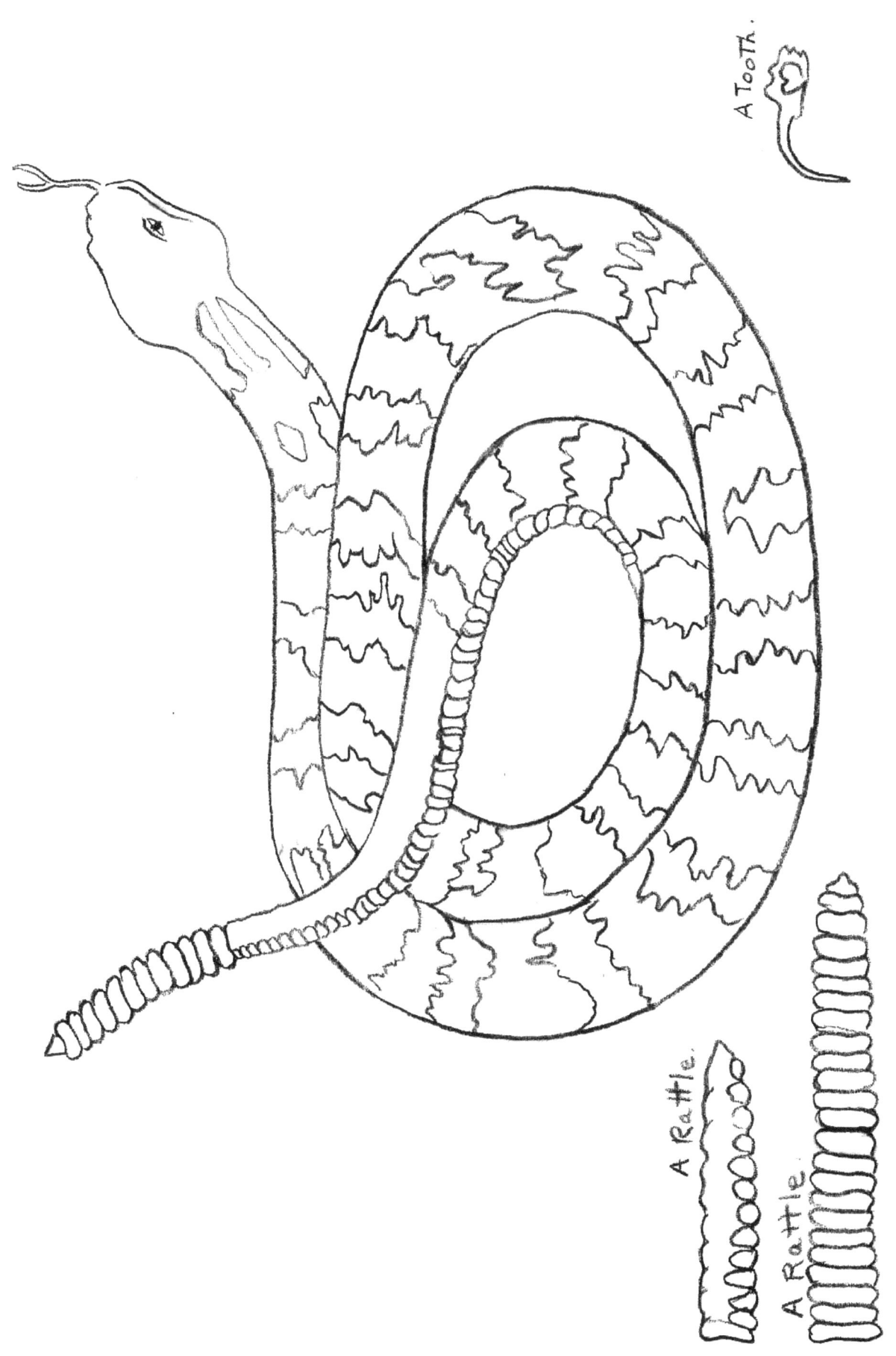

A Tooth.

A Rattle.

A Rattle.

Turdus Rhomboidalis

Turdus &c

Blue Tang & Coney

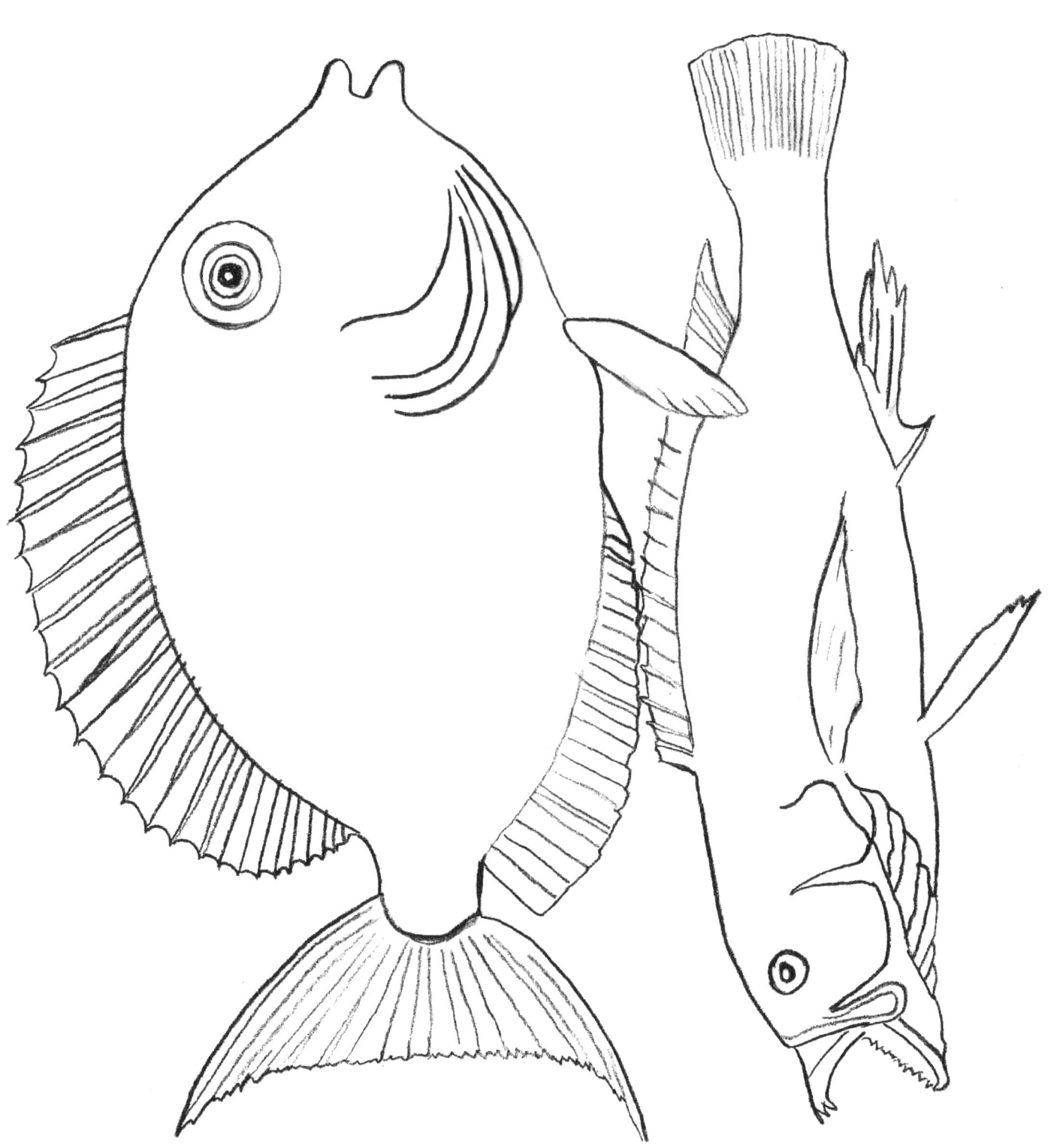

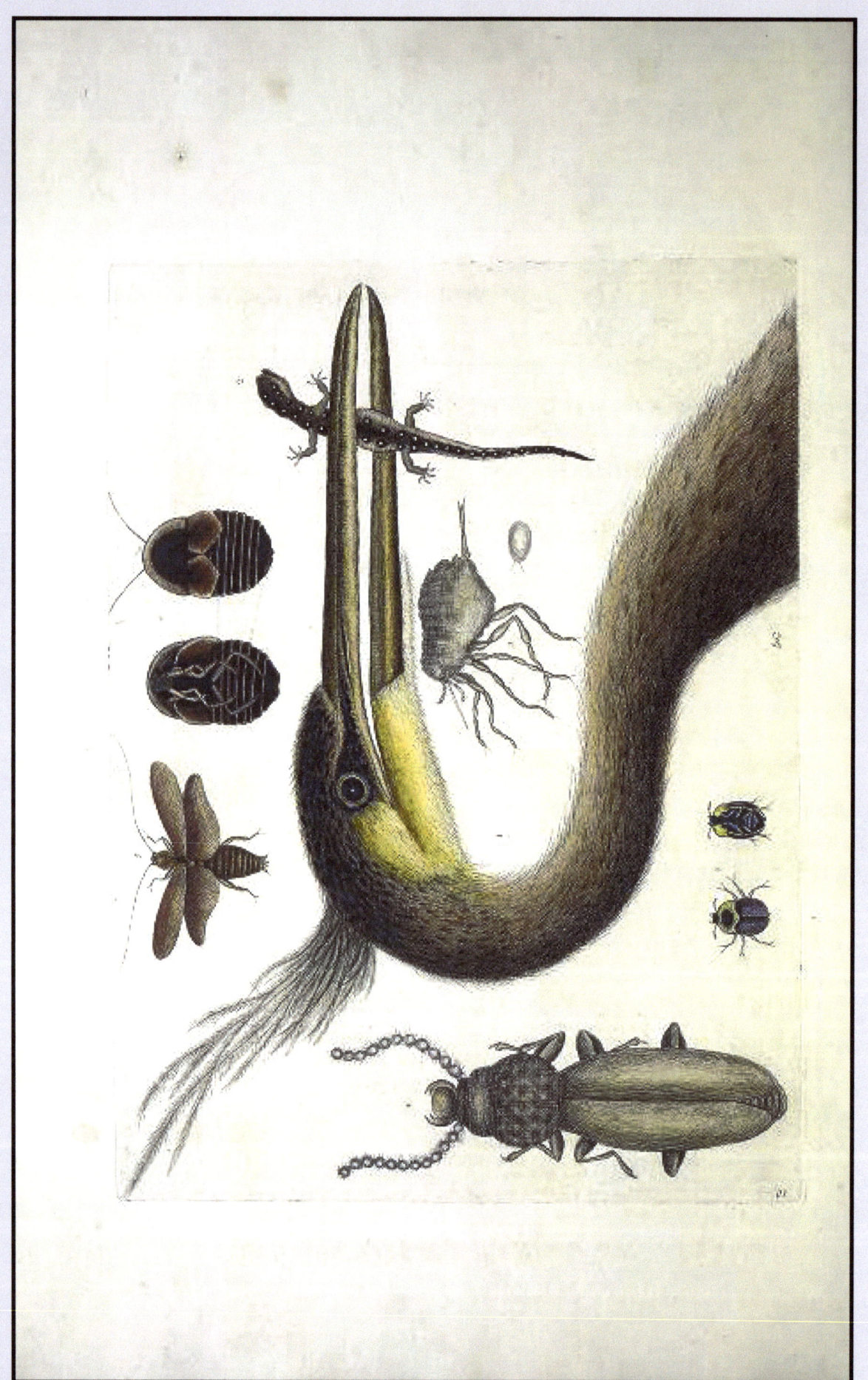

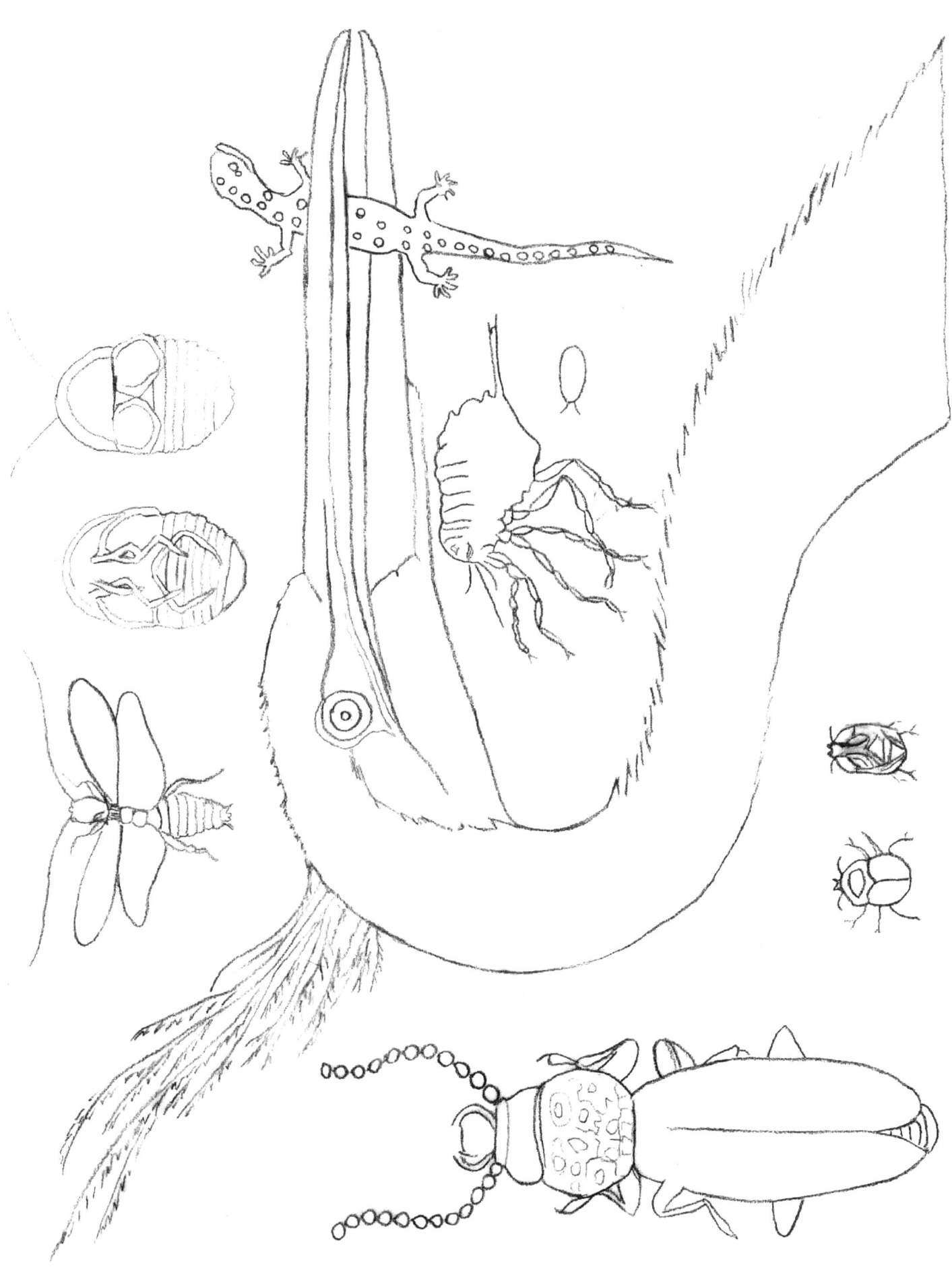

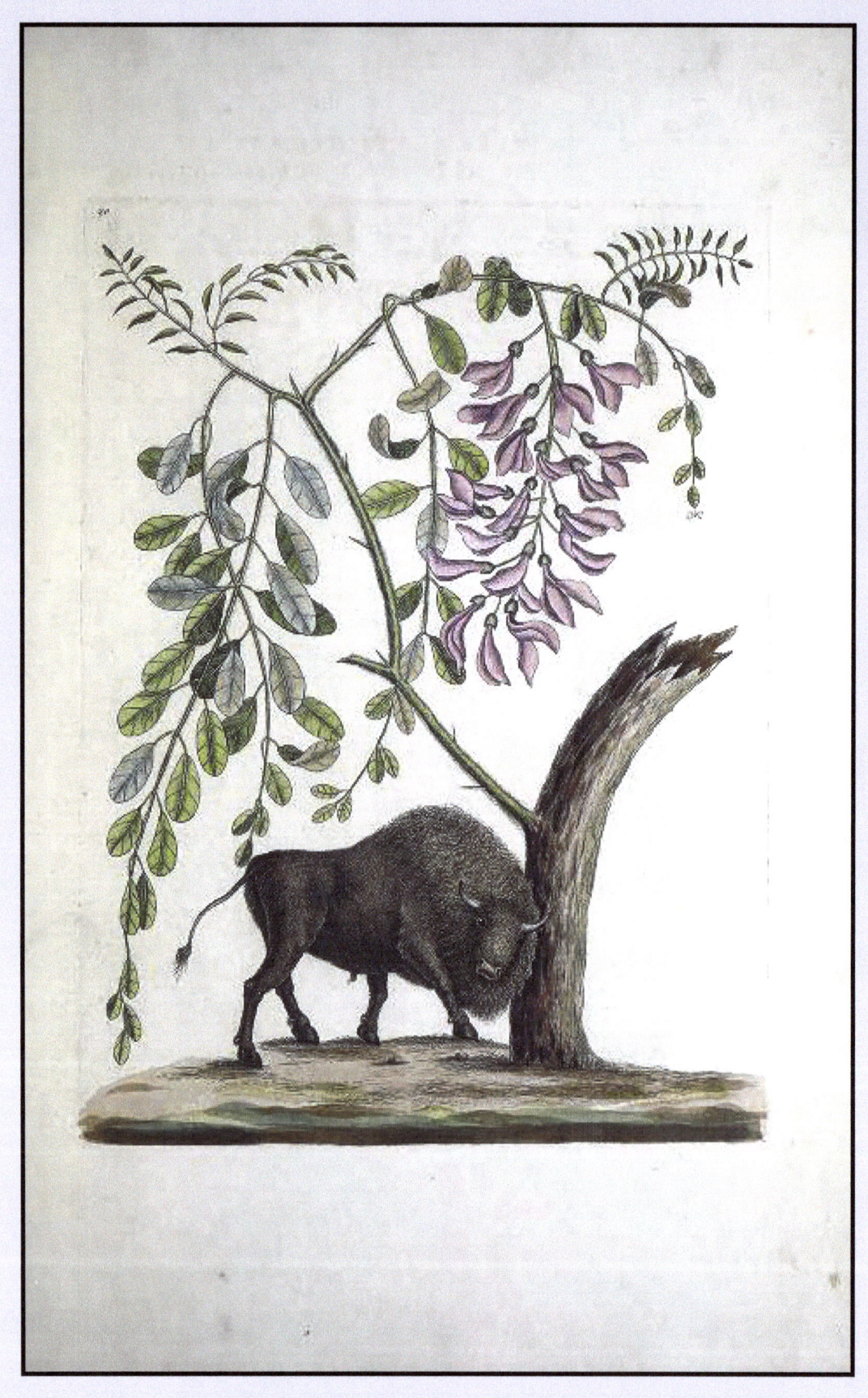

American Buffalo

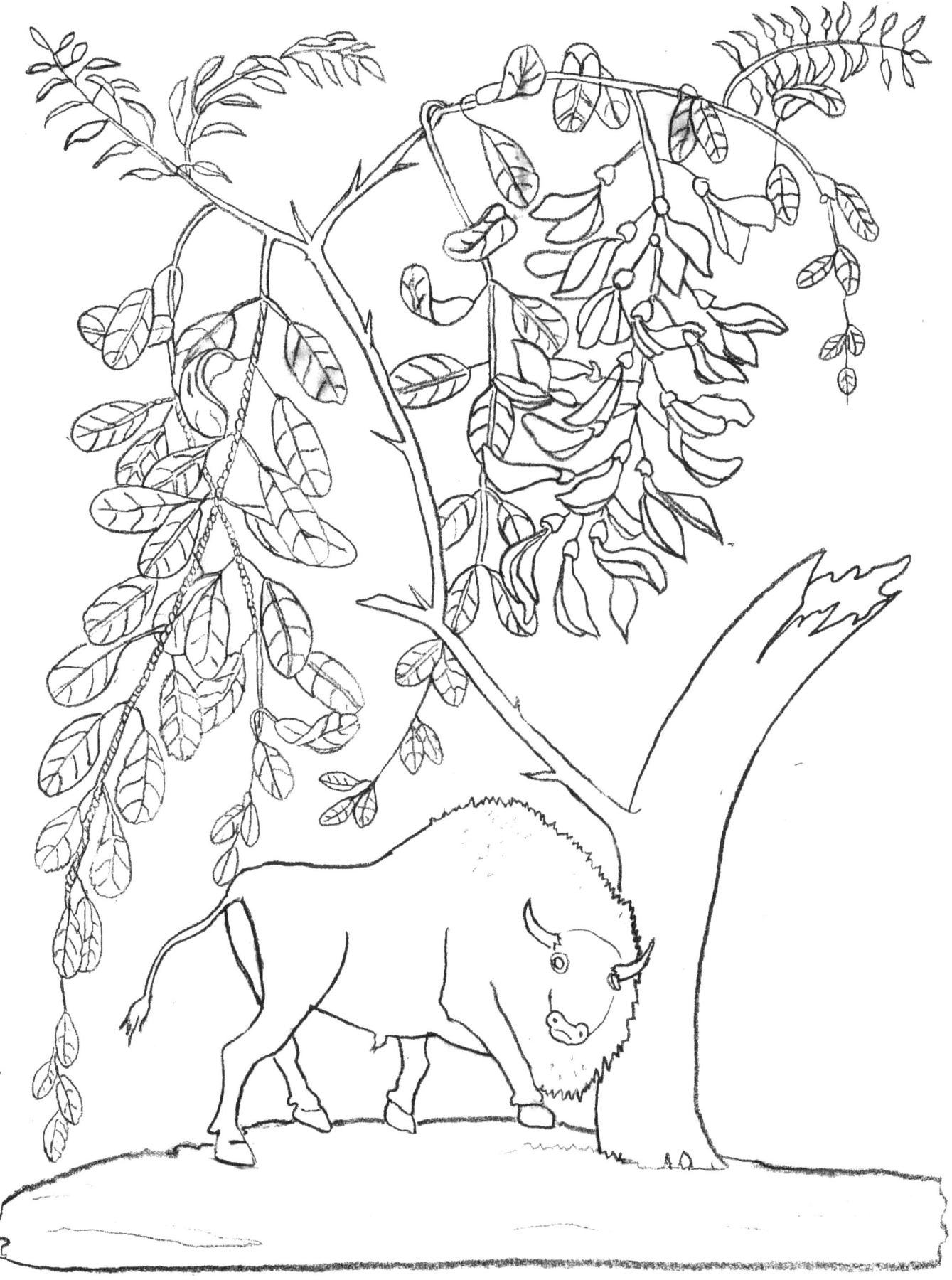

INFORMATION ABOUT THE CATESBY PRINTS

Page	Common Name*	The Natural History of South Carolina, Florida and the Bahama Islands**
Cover	Eastern screech-owl. (same for title page illustration)	Vol. 1 Plate 7
3, 4	Southern flying squirrel. American persimmon.	Vol. 2 Plate 76
6	Decorative drawing of Native American guide and gear.	Vol. 1 Page pi
7	Southern flying squirrel. Powdery strap airplant.	Vol. 2 Plate 77
	American Bald Eagle. Fish type is unknown.	Vol. 1 Plate 1
	Red Winged Blackbird. Southern bayberry plant.	Vol.1 Plate 13
	Bluejay. Laurel greenbrier plant.	Vol.1 Plate 15
	Pileated woodpecker. Live oak tree.	Vol.1 Plate 17
	Red headed woodpecker. Water oak tree.	Vol.1 Plate 20
	Mourning dove. Mayapple plant.	Vol.1 Plate 24
	Northern Cardinal. Mockernut hickory branch & nut. Small pignut (hickory).	Vol.1 Plate 38
	Eastern bluebird. Sarsaparilla vine.	Vol.1 Plate 47
	White cheeked pin-tail duck. Tree seaside tansy.	Vol.1 Plate 93
	White ibis. Goldenclub plant.	Vol.1 Plate 82
	Purple land crab. Blackwood plant.	Vol.2 Plate 32
	Hawksbill sea turtle and eggs.	Vol.2 Plate 39
	American Alligator, hatchling. Red mangrove tree.	Vol.2 Plate 63
	American bullfrog. Pink lady's-slipper plant.	Vol.2 Plate 72
	Common garter snake. Hammock viper's tail plant.	Vol.2 Plate 53
	Timber rattlesnake. Sample rattles and tooth.	Vol.2 Plate 41
	Blue tang fish. Coney fish.	Vol.2 Plate 10
	Great blue heron. Spotted salamander. Chigoe flea and egg. Beetle. American cockroach. Dubia cockroach. American carrion beetle.	Appendix Vol.2 Plate 10
	American buffalo or bison. Rose locust tree.	Appendix Vol.2 Plate 20

*Source: Nelson, E. Charles & Elliott, David J. (editors), For The Catesby Commemorative Trust, <u>Curious Mister Catesby: a "truly ingenious" naturalist explores new worlds.</u>

www.ingramcontent.com/pod-product-compliance
Lightning Source LLC
Chambersburg PA
CBHW040749200526
45159CB00025B/1810